MANIPUR
The Glorious Past

MANIPUR

The Glorious Past

A.K. Sharma

ARYAN BOOKS INTERNATIONAL
NEW DELHI

MANIPUR—The Glorious Past

Published in 1994 by :

ARYAN BOOKS INTERNATIONAL
4378/4B, Pooja Apartments
4, Ansari Road, Darya Ganj
New Delhi-110002, INDIA

ISBN-81-7305-050-3

Computer Typeset at Sriram Graphics, New Delhi.
Printed in India at Print Perfect, New Delhi.

To

Kusum

and

People of Manipur

Contents

Preface

In archaeological investigations North-East India has suffered neglect in spite of very hospitable climate and people. Some wrong notions have somehow been created in the minds of government officials and researchers about this beautiful archaeological treasure of the country. When the question of starting some work in the area comes the fear of inaccessibility, insurgency, difficult terrain and what not stalks the mind of the people resulting in reluctance to work in the area.

Knowing fully well that these false notions are deliberate creations of those few who wish to keep the area aloof from the growing activities of other parts of the country, the Prehistory Branch of the Archaeological Survey of India decided to devote more time in North-East India and dig out the evidences of its glorious past. Excavations at Sekta were the first step in this direction. The team was well received by the people particularly villagers and officials of the State Department of Archaeology and Museums who worked hard to make the joint endeavour a grand success. We were overwhelmed by the results of the excavations and spontaneous response of the scholars and commoners. But for the active interest taken by the Secretary, Culture, Government of India, Shri.Bhaskar Ghosh, Director General, Archaeological Survey of India, Shri M.C. Joshi and Dr.C.Margabandhu, Director (Explorations and Excavations) it would have been difficult to reach Imphal and achieve results as the entire team was provided air travel facilities by the Government.

As we selected Sekta for our operations devating from our original plan of digging at Salangthel, all the officials of the Ministry of Culture and Department of Archaeology and Museums, Government of Manipur extended spontaneous support and facilities to us. I am particularly grateful to Shri.S.Bheigya Singh, Superintendent and the ever ready colleagues of his department for their kind help in the excavations and in arranging the exhibition. But for missionary zeal of my colleagues S/Shri S.B.Ota. S.K.Lekhwani, N.G.Nikosey, R.K.Dwivedi, C.L.Yadav, Pyara Singh, N.K.Nimje, P.V.Janardhanan, V.W.Pathak and P.S.Pashine, it would have not been possible to undertake and complete the job in record time. I am also grateful to Shri Lokendra Arambam, Joint Director, Audio-Visual Research Centre, Manipur University,

Imphal for taking pains to videotape the entire excavations and findings for telecast in Doordarshan. I am also glad that the media. e.g. All India Radio, Imphal and local newspapers gave wide coverage to our entire work due to which things could reach to people in every walk of life. I am thankful to the Editor, *the India magazine* for publishing a detailed article titled 'Sekta the turning point' in their March, 1992 issue, with numerous photographs. Last but not the least to all those villagers, ladies, girls and boys of Sekta who provided us hospitality, residence and the required labour force during our stay in their village. It was a lifetime experience of cordiality everywhere, wherever we moved in Manipur. I wondered where is the difficult terrain, inhospitable climate, insurgency and all that of which so much propaganda has been deliberately made. A few months later we experienced the same atmosphere in Garo Hills of Meghalaya. My experience everywhere shows people love their past, everyone is eager to know more about it. I hope the beginning made by us would be followed up and that will be our reward.

After a few months, i.e. in October, 1991 when I again visited Sekta I was overwhelmed to find that Shri Bheigya Singh and his conservation colleagues have done wonderful job in preserving the site and finds in-situ in the form of first site museum of Manipur. Their efforts are worth emulation by others in the line. They should go and see for themselves where there is a will there is a way.

I shall be failing in my duties if I do not express my gratitude to research scholars S/Shri.B.Kulachandra Sharma, Gyaneshwar Singh and Mrs.Poornima Haorongbam who lived with us and worked day and night to make our excavations a grand success. For us Shri Ngangom Itocha Singh and his Annapoorna like wife Smt.Itocha Singh were god sent persons as it is they only who came forward and offered us the covered verandah of their house for our stay when we reached Sekta around sunset on twenty second of March 1991. We can never forget them. Personally for me it was a great experience of Manipur simplicity and hospitality. The ten feet by seven feet of space, covered with wattle and daub, with ice-cold stream of wind entering inside from holes here and there, the loud thud of torrential rains after sun set on the corrugated tin sheets and the cold floor were our companions in what comprised as our camp at Sekta. All these worldly inconveniences and the day's tiredness used to be wiped out from our faces, the moment steaming hot food used to be put before us by our *Aashryadata* (the one who gave us shelterd).

But for the voluntary offering of his land for our dig by Shri Hidam Gopal Singh, it would not have been possible for us to undertake the excavations. He and Sekta will always be in our memory. It was a new experience of mutual co-operation to work with S/Shri S.Bhaiya Singh, S.Rupoban Singh, Smt.Indrani Devi, N.Kumar Singh, K.Gunindro Singh, Ibomcha Singh, M.Ibomcha Singh, M.Bijoy Singh, Kh.Ibomcha Singh and W.Chaoba Singh. This was the team from State Archaeology. I express my profound thanks to the wonderful dare devil Senior photographer of the Survey Shri B.R.Rajput who accompanied me to Manipur during my first visit to the State in March 1990 and with whom I covered the rest of the places in Manipur and he photographed everything wonderfully.

I am also grateful to Shri.Samrendra Singh, and Smt.Kh. Sarojini Devi, who were Director Culture and Dy Director Archives and Museums, Govt.of Manipur, respectively due to whom my first visit to Manipur materialised. It was their keen interest in archaeology which culminated in excavations at Sekta.

I hope this small report will be of some use to the scholars and the students of Archaeology and History of the North-East.

A.K. Sharma

LIST OF ILLUSTRATIONS

Page

A. Figures

B. Plates

1. Introduction

Manipuris are very keen students of their history and culture, proud of what is known, eager and curious to discover and learn more. This became evident when during my first visit to Manipur in March 1990, I could see the burning desire amongst the officials of the State Department of Archaeology and Museums and amongst the free lance scholars and collectors of antiquity in the State to know more, about their unknown past. The only hindrance in their pursuit to know more about their past was the lack of archaeological evidences. This was not because it was not there but because they have not been brought to light through explorations and scientific excavations, partly due to lack of proper expertise and guidance and partly due to paucity of funds and infrastructure for such field works. Though from every quarter there is always emphasis that much more attention should be paid to the states of North-East India to bring them into the main stream of the country, hardly anything is being done in the field of archaeology, which holds the key to the glorious past of the region, when political, cultural and trade contacts were much more intimate between this remote part of the country and the rest of the mainland. Before the beginning of Christian era, there was free passages of people to and from the mainland. The most vital trade route from China to Afghanistan and further west passed through Manipur, Nagaland and Assam and people of these states played an active role in these activities. It is a pity that even after reorganisation of Circles of the Archaeological Survey of India and establishment of the headquarters of a separate Circle for North-East India at Gauhati, hardly any progress has been made in extending archaeological activities, both research and conservation, to various states of the region. Even in 1993, vital states like Mizoram and Manipur have hardly seen any archaeological activity by the A.S.I. In Manipur, there is only one centrally protected monument at Bishnupur, whereas in Mizoram there is none. In fact Mizoram is yet to find its place in the archaeological map of the country. It is not that there is dearth of dedicated workers for the area. The reason is lack of planning, firmness and proper incentives. Those who are interested to work in the area are snubbed for one reason or the other.

The work done as early as in 1835 by G.E. Westmorcott and discovery of stone tools in 1862 and researches by various dedicated scholars in the 19th century and first half of the 20th century, still continues to be the main source of archaeological material for the region. During the British period, archaeology of the region did not get much attention as due to the activities of Christian missionaries, the rulers were not interested in bringing out the glorious past of the people of the region before them as it would have proved a hindrance for spreading Christianity and resorting to mass conversion. This could be achieved by telling the people of the region that 'they are now being civilized from their state of barbarism, because they had no history and culture of their own'.

In the post-Independence era there was some response by some Archaeological Research Societies and University departments but their activities were concentrated mostly in Assam and some neighbouring areas. Manipur, Mizoram, Nagaland, Arunachal Pradesh, Meghalaya and Tripura still remained untouched though whatever work done, particularly in the field of prehistoric research, was by individual scholars like T.C.Sharma, O.K.Singh, R.V.Joshi, S.N.Rajguru, etc. In Manipur efforts made by the State department and individuals like Shri M.Gourachandra whose main collection of archaeological, anthropological and ethnological material was converted into Kakching People's Museum and Shri.Mutua Buhadir's collection of prehistoric tools in Mutua Museum, Imphal are commendable. Unfortunately so far no concerted efforts have been made by the Archaeological Survey of India either to explore or to excavate, on large scale, some archaeological sites in the region to provide the much needed data to reconstruct the history of Manipur. Excavations at Sekta by the author on behalf of Archaeological Survey of India was only a small effort in the direction but this was amply rewarded both in the form of excavation results and spontaneous positive response from the scholars, public, media and the State Government. A seminar and exhibition of Sekta finds was arranged at Imphal in collaboration with the State Department of Archaeology in April 1991 initially for three days (*Pl.IIA*). It was inaugurated by Padmashri Shri Khelchandra, the eminent scholar. The exhibition was opened by Shri M.K.Priyobratha Singh, Ex. Chief Minister, Manipur. Scholars, professors and students from all over the State participated in the seminar and expressed their views. They expressed their profound happiness and satisfaction on the results of the limited excavations and desired that more such excavations, seminars and exhibitions should be organised. They were happy that ultimately the Archaeological Survey of India came forward and fulfilled, partly, their long cherished desire. The response was so overwhelming that the exhibition had to be extended for a few more days. Even the Department of History, University of Manipur did not lag behind and I was requested by

Dr.Gangamumei Kabui, Professor and Head of the Department, to deliver a lecture on 'the Prehistoric Culture of Manipur including the excavations at Sekta', on 24-11-91. After the lecture there were searching questions from scholars and students.

BACKGROUND TO THE EXCAVATIONS

It all started in March, 1990, when I was asked by the then Jt. Director General, Shri.M.C.Joshi, to visit Imphal to examine the gold-masked human skulls recovered from near Imphal and from the slopes of the hill near Sekta(pl.I). They were unique and most outstanding finds. My main job was to examine the morphological characters of the skull and to give a report on the finds. I took advantage of my visit and cooperation of State authorities to visit some other areas and sites in Manipur.

After reaching Sekta, the mound on the left bank of Iril caught my imagination as it was in the vicinity of the hill slopes from where gold masked skulls and other antiquities were recovered. On enquiry I was told that the mound was a protected site of the State Department of Archaeology and Museums and that the department intended to excavate the site if permission is granted by the Archaeological Survey of India. Having firmly decided to do some archaeology in Manipur, when the opportunity would come, I departed. In 1991 this desire materialised and we reached Imphal in March 1991 with the intention to excavate the megalithic site of Salangthel near Bishnupur. But destiny took us to Sekta instead of Salangthel. After obtaining telephonic permission to change our plan from Salangthel to Sekta, as the Director General Shri. M.C.Joshi, was too eager to see that the site in Manipur is excavated, and after entering into an agreement with the State Department of Archaeology for joint excavation, we commenced our work on 22.3.1991.

As we had not brought our tents and camping equipments, we preferred to hire some accommodation in the village itself. Earlier we were warned to be careful as Sekta was the village from where terrorist activities in Manipur are supposed to have started. There was nothing for us to fear as we had come to unearth the past glory of Manipur and for that matter of India, our own. On reaching the village in dying hours of 22-3-91, we started to search for some accommodation. Our ever ready Manipuri friend Shri S.Bheigya Singh, Superintendent of Archaeology, Government of Manipur, could succeed in securing a small accommodation, hardly enough for seven of us to lie down rubbing each other, in the house of Shri Nganom Itocha Singh. As we settled down, shivering in the cold and spreading the poor matting spared by the State Archaeology to us to be used as bed along with our sleeping bags, my enthusiastic colleagues S/Shri R.K.Dwivedi, N.K.Nimje and C.L.Yadav managed for our food with the helping hand of the lady of the house Smt.Itocha

Singh, who proved a Lakshmi for us for the entire period of our stay, thanks to her, we never felt we were away from home except for the arrows of cool winds that used to pierce through the crevices of the bamboo matting that covered the verandah to convert it into a room like accommodation. We had even to borrow utensils, some clothes and purchase afresh our digging kits as our entire luggage was held up at Dumdum air port in Calcutta due to sudden cancellation of flights. Visits to Imphal Airport with hopes for arrival of our entire luggage became a regular job for our ever-ready storekeeper Shri C.L.Yadav. Indian Airlines were bent upon testing our patience. We had to manage our field work mainly with women as except one or two men others were not willing to work. It is not that they were engaged elsewhere, but simply because they were not habituated to do physical labour for others. This field is for women who are very sincere, honest and hard working. After initial difficulties, which we generally encounter everywhere in the beginning with new hands, everything was smooth. They quickly understood what we wanted. Once they understood the value and delicate nature of our job, they were very cautious and careful. During the entire period of work in the trenches and thereafter in the camp we were surrounded by people, particularly young boys with eager eyes to know something more. Though the boys were not ready to work on payment, but they were always too ready to rush and bring things for us from our camp or elsewhere. This shows they are not lazy but had been moulded by tradition from generations to relax as in Manipur male children get more care than their female counter part. During the entire period of our stay we got taste of only love and care. I and my friends wondered where was the much publicised terrorism and the terrorists. After the news of our discoveries were broadcast by All India Radio, Imphal and circulated through local Manipuri Newspapers, the villagers looked at us with pride and respect. Their village, their State, was in the news. We will be and for that matter Archaeological Survey of India will be missing a golden opportunity to encash on the goodwill and enthusiasm of the Manipuris to bring them closer to the mainstream. More such excavations and exhibitions are the need of the time. This also holds good for Nagaland, Mizoram, Arunachal Pradesh, Tripura and Meghalaya. I hope the opportunity will not be lost to bring to light the hidden past of the people of North-East India, which was definitely glorious and not dark as our colonizers taught us.

Students from the Department of History, University of Manipur under the leadership of Smt.Dr.L.Kunjeswari Devi, took advantage of the excavations and actively participated in the field work. This was their first chance do actual practical work in the field. They could feel the difference between theories taught in classrooms and actual field work outside (*Pl.IIB*).

Manipur occupies a pivotal place in the development of man but due to lack of proper investigation evidences have not yet come to light, as they should have. There are a number of caves and rock shelters in the hills of Manipur which might have been the shelters for the prehistoric man. One such group of caves, Khangkhui caves located near Khangkhui, a Tangkhul Naga village, at a distance of eleven kms. south-east of Ukhrul, was excavated by O.K.Singh. It yielded evidences of Late Stone age. These finds have been compared to the Kurnool finds dating back to around 3000 B.C. Neolithic tools and pottery have been reported from Tharon caves, 4 kms. north of village Tharon, a Liangmei Naga village, on the banks of Kalem-ki-magu. These are sandstone formations. From Napachik, a small hillock near the Meitei village of Wangu in the southern part of the Imphal valley, located on the right bank of Manipur river neolithic tools have been recovered. TL dating of potsherds from Napachik and Nongpok are 3450 B.P.(PRL-TL79) and 4460 ± B.P. (B.S.523), respectively. A large number of stray finds in the form of edge-grounded and fully grounded stone tools have been collected from Tangkhul, Ukhrul and Thoubal areas. Thsese collections in the museums and with individuals were, as far as possible, studied by the Prehistory Branch of the Archaeological Survey of India, in October, 1991. They were found to be very similar to Neoliths from Sikkim, Darjeeling area, West Bengal and Orissa, smaller in size and having pointed or narrow rounded butts (Pl. III A). The percentage of the much publicised shouldered celts was very low, only a few tools of this type in a vast collection of nearby 600 tools from different locations and in the possession of different agencies. This evidence clearly demolishes the earlier held theory that the Neolithic culture of North-East was deeply influenced by the Neolithic culture of Burma and South-East Asia. Even in T.C.Sharma's collection from Assam, and Meghalaya and other collections housed in the State Museum, Kohima, the number of shouldered celts is limited. It is evident that the Neolithic culture in North-East was closely linked to similar culture in other parts of Eastern India. The occasional contacts with Burma and far East were definitely there but they were never ancestral to the Neotithic culture of the East and North-East India.

As the drying up of lakes in the valley started some time around 10,000 years back all the stone age sites are found on the hill tops. Most of the Neolithic sites discovered so far are on the slopes of hills. Not a single site has been found, so far, in the valley itself as during Neolithic times the valley was either occupied by lake waters or wherever it had receded, the exposed land was unfit for human occupation due to its marshy nature (Sharma 1986). The post neolithic period experienced considerable erosion on the slopes of the surrounding hills of the Manipur basin probably as a result of human interference with nature.

It is only after the lakes had receded considerably towards the southern side, the vast stretch of marshy land dried up and suitable drainage pattern through the exposed land emerged, the valley became fit for occupation and cultivation. (*Pl. IV*) This appears to have happened around the middle of the first millennium B.C. As such it was thought desirable to search for archaeological sites of early historical period along the banks of the newly formed rivers. A number of sites were located on the banks of Iril river in 1991. As our dig was progressing at Sekta revealing burials with scores of antiquities before the glare of visitors, people understood the importance of these hidden objects. It created awareness amongst the people about the need to protect and preserve these things of the past which belonged to their forefathers. The immediate advantage of keeping everything open was that on 6th April, 1991, in an adjoining village called Pungdongbam, situated on the left bank of River Ril Turel while digging in his courtyard Shri Sagol Sem Khamba came across a number of huge conical earthern jars buried in the soil. These jars contained iron and copper objects and beads similar to that found at Sekta (*Pl. IIIB*). As he had observed our excavations and seen us carefully collecting these objects, realising their importance, he immediately came to us and informed about his findings. I visited the spot immediately and to my great surprise found that his entire courtyard and the kitchen garden area was full of pot burials. There were very large seized conical storage jars containing plenty of iron and copper objects and beads of varieties. These jars, in black and red, were much bigger in size than those found at Sekta. They also contained fragments of human bones. There was no doubt that there was another site with a burial mound just 3 kms. away from Sekta, again on the bank of a river. As larger part of the mound was already destroyed earlier, while constructing a house, from where also similar objects were found, but were destroyed as at that time they never knew their historical value and importance, the only course left was to record the things. The antiquities were collected by the State Department of Archaeology. This was the positive aspect of our efforts at Sekta but at Sekta itself we were mute witnesses to the negative aspect. We had already located atleast five more mounds in addition to the mound of our operations. Surface indications were that they are also burial mounds. I was inclinded to dig some trenches atleast in one or two of them to find out whether they were similar to the mound which we were digging, in contents and Period or there was any difference. But the owners of the lands in whose jurisdiction the mounds were located, suspecting that the their mounds may also be subjected to investigations by us, one fine morning called bulldozers and got these mounds wiped out from the topography of the village. During bulldozing operations, scores of pottery, iron and copper objects and beads were picked up by the children and by the persons from the State Department of Archaeology and History department of University of Manipur. In spite of my repeated requests to the concerned State officials they could not do anything to stop deliberate destruction of the sites of great archaeological importance which were likely to throw more light on the lesser known early history of Manipur. I could not understand as to why the Government was only a helpless witness. If things in Manipur are allowed to continue like this, I doubt, in few years, anything worth of archaeological importance would be left and Manipur's history will remain in dark. I am not prepared to believe that the people could not be persuaded not to destroy such mounds and sites. Even though some section of the people are hostile and do not wish to change certain pre-conceived notions about their history, a little courage and effort will be able to convince them for future investigations. The scene of destruction was the saddest moment in my life. We do not know how many sites, monuments and sculptures are being wiped out in our country everyday, partly due to utter neglect on our part and partly due to mad rush for urbanisation and industrialisation and above all our dam building mania. In the submergence areas of Tehri dam, Sardar Sarovar, Nagarjuna sagar,, Ghosikhurd and scores of mini and major dams, apart from colossal loss of forest covers and villages, there is tremendous impact on eco-system and drainage patterns apart from loss of hundreds of archaeological sites from Prehistoric times to medieval. As every inch or our country is dotted with sites, it hardly pinches us if a few hundred of them are lost. Let us see from the point of view of other western countries who are starving for such sites. Atleast in North-East India where hardly any archaeological field research has been done so far to lift the cover of darkness from the shining layers of the past, it would be better if such destructions are kept to the minimum.

On 5-10-1991, during our visit to the People's Museum, Kakching, district Thoubal, Shri M.Gourachandra, the lone curator of the museum, showed antiquities recovered from near a hill at Panajopalum Ching. They included two gourd shaped handmade jars, a black ware bowl containing human lower jaw along with two carnelian beads, one quartz bead, one copper bangle (decorated) and one copper lid of a pot. (PLs. *V & VI*). These antiquities were recovered while digging earth for the nearby college building. A visit to the actual find spot revealed it to be a site almost similar to Sekta.

About 6 kms. from Kakching in village Laimanai there are twin mounds from where handmade pottery and neolithic stone tools were recovered. This is a promising site, almost in the valley, down the foothills. To the south-west of Laimanai there is another village by name Langmeidong where also a huge mound, full of potsherds could be located. These sites indicate that the entire Manipur valley is dotted with ancient sites.

2. The Site

Thumkhong Lairembi. Sekta (Long 94^0 24'N, Lat.24^0 35'24"E) in district Imphal is located 18 kms. north-east of Imphal on the left bank of river Iril, a tributary of Imphal and Manipur rivers. (Fig. 1) As per evidence available, Sekta, atleast a couple of centuries before the beginning of Christian era, was a sprawling habitational site. Now due to heavy ploughing almost the entire habitational area has been destroyed with patches of 35 to 40 cms of deposit left at some places. On the east and north, the village is surrounded by low lying hills called Thumkhong Ching(hill of salt water spring). In fact hardly a century back there was a big salt water lake on the top of this hill. The entire requirement of common salt of the nearby area was met from the salt from this lake. Due to deforestation of the hills leading to depletion in the catchment area and heavy silting of the lake, the lake has become shallow and almost dried out. Salt precepitation has totally stopped.

On 4.9.1989, from the slopes of Thumkhong Ching hills facing village Sekta an oval shaped bell-metul container was dug up by the shepherds grazing their herds. The container contained a human skull (*Pl. XI*) of a male of about 45 years of age with pronounced nasal bone and broad receding forehead along with the sheets of silver used for covering the skull, greenish glass beads and two necklaces made of glass and coral beads. Inquiries revealed that some time back three or four more skulls with containers were dug up by villagers but they could not be retrieved. The author visited the area on 4-3-90 to examine the find spot. A survey of the hill revealed some more interesting features. On the top of the hill a rock shelter now filled up with debris was located (*Pl. XII*). The shelter is still under worship by local people as could be seen from the presence of an iron *Trishul* at the mouth of the shelter. The top of the hill is a flat area where some structural remains of hoary antiquity were noticed.

Just below the findspot of bronze container with skull a sprawling habitational mound with nearly 0.70 m deposit was located. The mound is sprinkled with handmade red ware with reed and mat impressions. (*Pl. XIII*)

During excavations in March-April, 1991, while taking the students of the Department of History, University of Manipur on an exploration trip, on

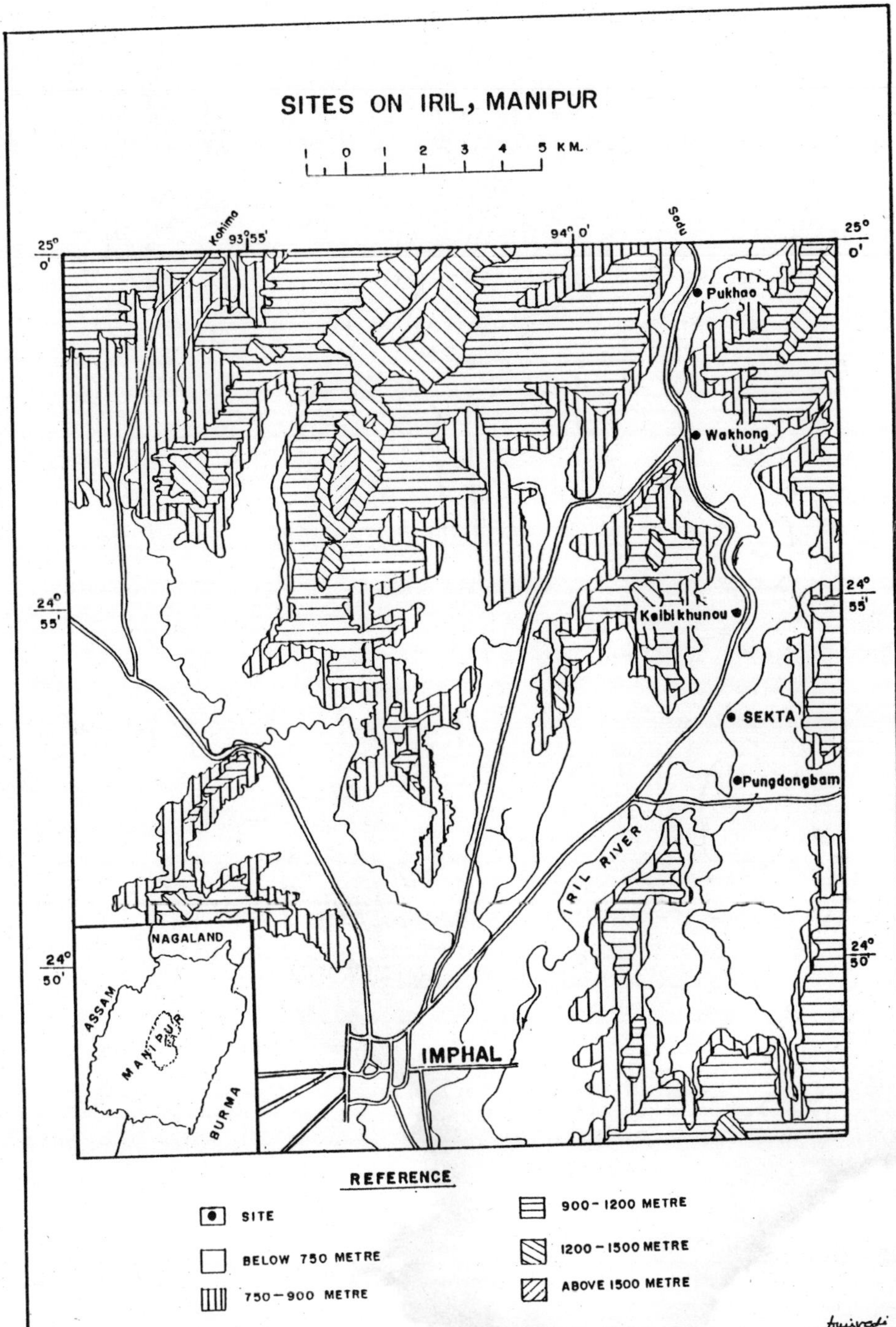
SITES ON IRIL, MANIPUR
1 0 1 2 3 4 5 KM.
Kohima
93°55'
94° 0'
Sadu
25° 0'
24° 55'
24° 50'
Pukhao
Wakhong
Keibikhunou
SEKTA
Pungdongbam
IRIL RIVER
IMPHAL
NAGALAND
ASSAM
MANIPUR
BURMA
REFERENCE
SITE
BELOW 750 METRE
750 – 900 METRE
900 – 1200 METRE
1200 – 1500 METRE
ABOVE 1500 METRE

Fig. 1

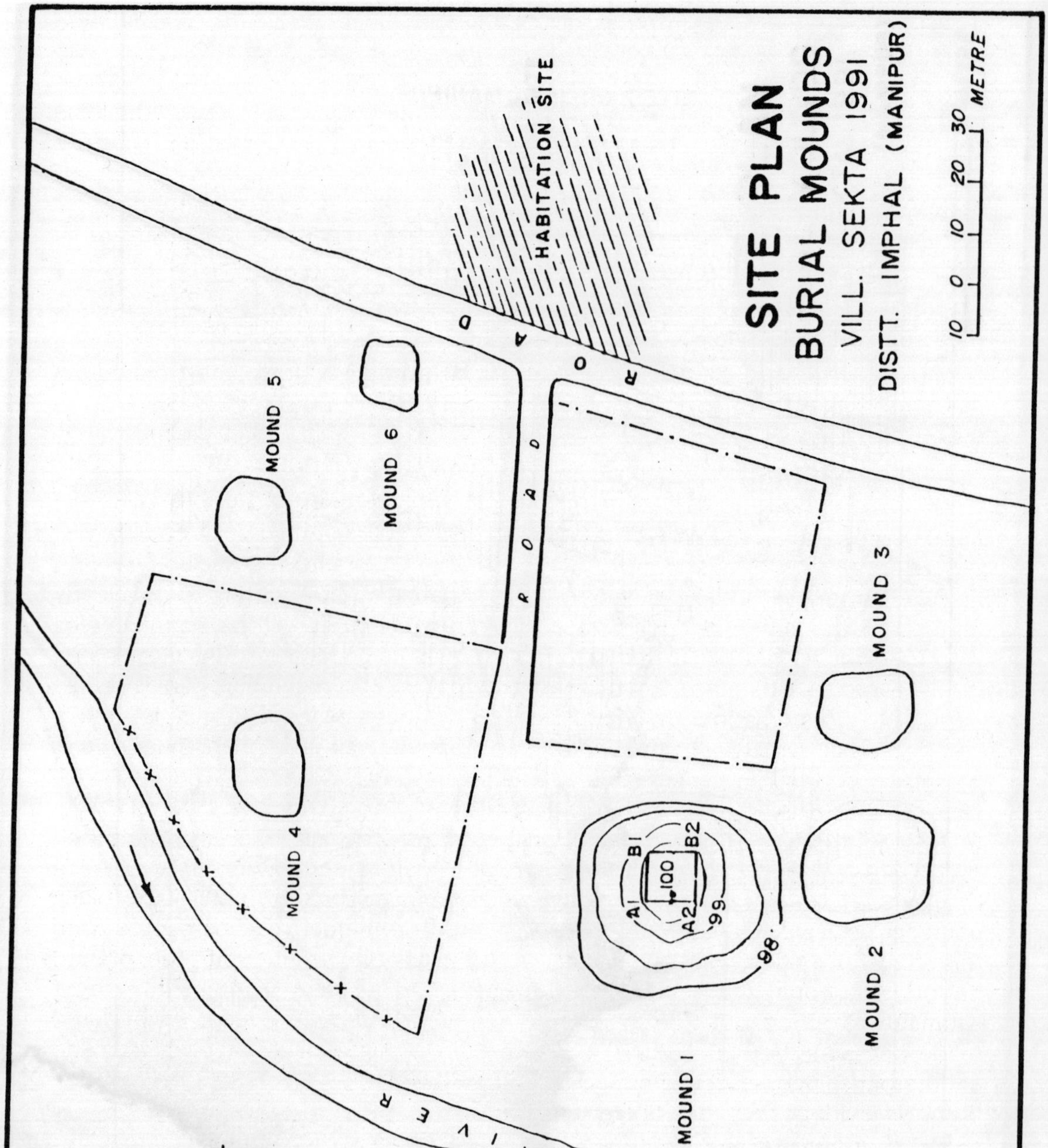
SITE PLAN
BURIAL MOUNDS
VILL. SEKTA 1991
DISTT. IMPHAL (MANIPUR)
10 0 10 20 30 METRE
HABITATION SITE
ROAD
ROAD
MOUND 1
MOUND 2
MOUND 3
MOUND 4
MOUND 5
MOUND 6
A1
A2
B1
B2
100
99
98
IRIL RIVER
N

Fig. 2

6-4-91 to the north of the above mentioned mound at the foothills an anthropomorphic figure made out of Himalayan schist was located (*Pl. XIVA*). The figure 0.85 m. tall, 0.045 m. wide at the base, 0.33 m wide at the top and 0.20m wide in the centre occupies the centre of a small hilllock. The figure has a squarish cross-section throughout. Its central portion has been finely polished like neolithic tools. As per the legends 'if any person touches it, that evening is bound to witness thunderstorm and rain'. The anthropomorphic figure appears to have been carved and erected during neolithic times, but this needs confirmation.[1]

From various evidences in and around Sekta it is clear that from remote past the village was selected for habitation by people.

In the village itself there were atleast six visible mounds, all situated on the left bank of Iril and all appear to be burial mounds (Fig. 2). Out of these the one nearest to the river and protected by the State Archaeology Department was selected for excavation (*Pl. XV*).

It is a slow rising mound with nearly 3.00 metres of deposit over the natural soil. The river flows in the west and habitational area is mostly located to the east of the burial mounds. The entire habitational area of the past has been brought under cultivation. A look into the surrounding areas clearly marks out the difference. The area with grey colour is the habitational area whereas that with whitish fine silt is the virgin area. Moreover, the grey area is full of potsherds and a few antiquities whereas the remaining part is totally devoid of pottery and ashy deposits. The natural soil of the area is yellow compact clay devoid of any extraneous material. Similar phenomenon was witnessed at Gufkral (a neolithic site in Jammu and Kashmir). The yellowish clay has the property of getting easily levigated. Moreover it has the elasticity to be easily moulded into different shapes. This clay has been mostly utilised by the first settlers of Sekta who turned wheel made pottery. In course of time, after the denudation of forests, when the river brought with it the black compact clay mixed with extraneous material from higher reaches people used this clay for pottery making. Being most unsuitable for the purpose due to impurities, people had to discard the wheel and resort to handmade pottery. Ultimately in course of time wheel made pottery was totally replaced by hand made ones. As the handmade wares are definitely inferior to their wheel made counterparts, people could have reached to the depths of original yellow clay but it is evident they did not do so for two reasons- a) wheel made pottery required more wood for proper firing, but due to fast cutting of trees for converting the areas into fields, enough wood was not easily available nearby and (b) it appears, people were not prepared to put labour.

---

1. Almost a similar stone anthropomarphic figure is standing in Andamans, Near Port Blair, with inscriptions (*Pl. XIVB*)

3. Geology and Environment

Manipur State situated at the eastern corner of India lies between Lat.23^0 47'N and 25^{0}41'N and Long. 93^{0}6'E and 94^{0}48'E.

It has two physical divisions--the flat alluvial valley and the hilly tracts surrounding the valley (*Pl. XVI*). The hilly tract covers almost 90% of the total area. The hill ranges of Manipur form a part of the Himalayan Mountain system. In fact in remote past the entire area was a shallow lake or sea called Tethys. The lake received sediments eroded from the Archaen rocks during the Palaeozoic and Mesozoic periods. During the Cretaceous period North-East India underwent organic movement caused by geodynamic forces. The long accumulated sediments on the floor of the Tethys were deformed as ridges and basins. This caused the appearance of land on the one hand and deepening of parts of the Tethys on the other. The organic earth movements producing tectonic highlights, ridges and basins were followed by periods of quiescence, prolonged erosion and deposition on an enormous scale-sediments were deposited shrinking geosynclinal shelf or newly formed lakes and lagoons. Oldest rocks found in eastern Manipur belong to Cretaceous group, including shales, slates, siltstones and quartzite. The limestones of Cretaceous group occur near Ukhrul and Humdung where cave formations have taken place. These caves have proved on the basis of archaeological evidence to be abodes of Prehistoric men of Manipur. In Manipur there are north-south parallel hill ranges going upto 3050 m. above sea level. The hill ranges are higher in the eastern parts than in the west. It falls into the humid land form area.

In the remote past the entire Manipur valley was a big lake (*Pl. XVII*). The Imphal plain was formed due to the uplift in the southern mountain which led to the reversal of the drainage system and impounding of water in the area where there are now lakes and swamps. The average elevation of the valley is 763 m. 600 square km. area is occupied by lakes and marshes e.g. Loktak, Ikop-pat, Waithou-pat, Kharung-pat, Pumlet-pat, Lamjo-pat and Lousi-pat, etc. The process of silting of lake started much before 25,000 years. The Loktak lake probably represents a remnant of once a large lake which was carrying greater volume of water sometimes during the Quaternary. Evidences of changes in lake levels were observed in the dug out trenches in the Loktak hydroelectric project area and at Singda dam site. The deep drilling in Loktak lake has revealed that there is a peaty clay deposit of more than 36 metre in the area. The deposit at the depth of 12 m. has been dated to 25000±660 B.P. (B.S.-147) whereas the deposit from upper levels (35 cm.to 40 cm) has been dated to 7980 -- 470 B.P. (B.S.±194) (Singh, 1983). Fluvio-lacustral clays occur a few metres above the present aggreded surface, while fluvial gravels alternate with fluvio-lacustral clays at 3 to 5 metre and loam levels below the surface. Besides, carbonaceous clays are found to alternate with greyish, at times ferruginized (suggestive of the drying up of the lake) clays. These geomorphic features definitely suggest changes in the water budget of the lake during the Quaternary.[1]

As the lake started receding towards north, the valley has a north-south slope. Almost all the rivers of Manipur except the Leimatak, flow from north to south. The central plain of Manipur being the flood plain of rivers that drain it, it has thick deposits of sands, clays and silts of fluvio-lacustrine origin with their usual characteristics. The Barak River, the longest river, starting from a point in northern hills flows into western and southern hills then into the Cachar and the Suema valleys of Bangladesh. The Irang and the Makru of the Tamenglong area flow into the great Barak. The Imphal or Manipur River (Minno of Ptolemy) traverses the valley of Manipur, starting from the hills to the north of the valley, flowing through the Chin hills and then joins the Chindwin in Burma. The Imphal, the Iril, the Thoubal, the Nambol rivers which run across the valley are dotted with a number of archaeological sites of different periods, some known and many still to be brought to light. Today these rivers, their banks and their fertile flood plains provide livelihood to the people who populate the river banks. The Barak and the Jiri rivers in the west are navigable for a considerable distance. In the hills on the west bank of the Barak River there is a group of lakes known as the Zeilad. Iril, a tributary of Imphal River rises in the Lamkui and Kadam hills of the n-e-Mao. After flowing southwards it joins the Imphal River at Lilong. Its catchment area is 1260 sq.kms., average bed slope is 1:4200. It has a maximum discharge of 398.77 cusecs and minimum discharge is 0.861 cusecs.

As per studies conducted by R.V. Joshi and S.N. Rajguru, etc. in 1978-79, 'there is no geological evidence of Quaternary glacial or Periglacial climate upto an elevation of about 1500 m. above Mean Seal Level. In fact ferruginous (oxidized) cement and matrix of gravel formations suggest sub-tropical climate during the Quaternary. In the source region of Imphal valley, 50 kms. due north of Imphal city, gravel fill (20 to 30 m. thick) cone terraces are present at 1200 m, 1000 m. and 900 m. above M.S.L. comparable to those observed in the Banganga and Sirsa valleys in Himachal Pradesh. These gravel fill

1. Indian Archaeology-1978-A Review, R.V. Joshi, S.N. Rajguru, etc. p.29.

surfaces are the products of colluvio-alluvial processes characteristic of a mountainous region. The hill ranges surrounding the Imphal valley rise upto 3000 m. above M.S.L. and steep slopes of these high hills have favoured fairly thick formations of colluvio-alluvial gravels. The present course of Imphal River cuts through these gravel terraces. Neither stone tools nor animal and plant fossils were discovered in the gravels exposed in the road sections. The present Imphal river meanders through a vast aggregated plain of fluvio-lacustral origin.

Among the minerals available in Manipur are iron ore, copper ore, rock salt and limestone. The occurrence of iron ore is limited only to a few localities in the Imphal valley and near the border town of Moreh in the eastern hills. Copper ore is explored near Ukhrul. Chromite is found in the Shiroi hills of Ukhrul. Lignite mixed with clay is found at Kangvai. Small quantities of nickel and cobalt associated with copper ores are found at Nangu and Kongal Thana areas.

SOILS

1. Non Laterized Red Soil (Ultisol):

The eastern and western hills are having non-laterized red soil having red or yellowish red brown colour depending on the presence of hydrated oxides of iron. They have been mainly derived from weathered sandstone/slate sandstone, slate and phyllite. They are moderate to highly acidic and contain a fair quantity of nitrogen, phosphate and potash.

2. Laterized soil (Oxisol):

This is available predominantly in the Barak valley and the hill slopes of western hills. It is red, coarse and acidic, rich in potash, nitrogen and phosphates.

3. Alluvial (Entisol):

This is normally deposited by rivers. It is clayey loam in texture, grey to brown in colour, moderate to less acidic. It contains potash, phospates, nitrogen and organic matter.

4. Organic soil (Histosol):

It is of hydromorphic origin and is found in mud around lakes, marshes and low lying areas. It is found in the form of clayey loam and is dark grey in colour, rich in organic matter and highly acidic. It has a good proportion of nitrogen and phosphate but is poor in potash.

FLORA

The hills of Manipur are covered with dense forests. A few hundred years ago the valley was also covered with forests and swamps which have now been denuded. They could be seen, now, only in the form of groves surrounding the villages. In 1835 R.B. Pemberton wrote "I know no spot in India in which the products of forests are so varied and magnificent but their utility is entirely local". Half a century later in 1886, E.W. Dun saw almost the same plentiful forests. He wrote, "The climate once rainy and temperate covers the hills in the western portion with thick forests and induces the inhabitants to grow rice, causes numerous rivers, streams and marshes, and encourage aquatic and water loving plants. Oak replaces bamboo, firs for Nageshwar, a drier climate produced a lighter and different kind of jungle".

Manipur being in the monsoon belt of South-East Asia is included in the same ecosystem of the forests of the region. The flora of Manipur has been identified with the flora of Assam hills. F. Kingdom Ward, the famous Botanist writes "Some ten thousand years ago, the climate of Manipur, as of all eastern India, was far more colder than it is today. The vegetation must have been different, and no less so the forest. Ten thousand years ago the flora of the whole northern hemisphere was still struggling in the grip of the ice age during which the Himalayas were heavily iced and glaciers were formed. This led to the migration of northern flora to the south. For long ages Manipur was almost completely sterile. As the climate improved plant refugees began to return to their old homes from the warmth of south, from the deep valleys and plains."

Of the various species of plants, teak, the Khasia pine, bamboo, the agar and wild tea plants are worth mentioning. The most distinguished flora is the famous Sirohility (*Lilium macklennia*).

RAINFALL AND CLIMATE

The climate of Manipur during late Pleistocene was subtropical but drier than that of today. Both climate and tectonics played an important role in shaping the landscape of the area. It now falls into humid land form area. It has mainly three seasons. Winter from December to February, Summer from March to April and hot and rainy from May to September. The coldest month is January when temperature goes down to 12.65^{0}C. The average rain fall is 1673 mm. with the number of rainy days being 152.

As per Rajguru's observations "Shrinking of lakes in Kashmir and Manipur and excessive stripping of hill slopes in the Garo hills of Meghalaya are strongly suggestive of weakening of south-west monsoon and comparatively active winter monsoon in the major part of India north of 22^0 latitude".

TRADE ROUTES

Sir Arthur Phayre observes that according to the traditions among the Burmese, the present remains and the names of the cities, render it probable that easy communication existed between the Gangetic India and Tagaung, and trade was carried on through Eastern Bengal and Manipur.[1] The existence of such a route in the second century B.C. has been hinted at by Pelliot. According to him there was a regular trade route by land between Eastern India and China through Upper Burma and Yunan.[2] Through this route Indians came and established their political power in upper Burma and the mountainous regions of the upper valleys of Irawadi, the Salween, the Mekongal, the Red River as far as Yunan.[3] The oldest land route between India and China was probably through Assam, Upper Burma, and Yunan. Chinese cotton and bamboo were carried through this route from China to Bactria via India.[4] P.C.Bagchi says that this Assam-Burma route to China started from Pataliputra, passed through Campa (Bhagalpur), Kajangal (Rajmahal) and Pundravardhana (North Bengal) and went to Kamarupa (Gauhati). From Assam three routes went to Burma; one through the valley of Brahmaputra upto Patkai range and then through the passes upto upper Burma; the second through Manipur upto the Chindwin valley; and the third through the Arakan upto Irrawaddy valley. These three routes met on the frontier of Burma near Bhamo, and then proceeded over mountains and across river valleys to Yunan fu. According to Phayre in early times contact between Gangetic India and Tagaung lay through Manipur.

Mc Cosh refers to no less than five roads leading from Sadiya, the frontier station of the Brahmaputra valley into Tibet or China proper.[5] They are : (i) The pass of the Dihong, (ii) the Mishmi route, (iii) The Phungas pass to Muncher and China, (iv) the route by Manipur to the Irrawaddy, and (v) the Patkai pass to Buama on the Irrawaddy.

R.C. Majumdar writes, "The Indians also proceeded to the Far East by land routes through Bengal, Manipur and Assam. They reached lower Burma through Arakan, and upper Burma through ravine passes in the Patkai range or Manipur hills. As already noted Chinese wares passed through land routes from Yunan and Szechuan to northern India in the second century B.C. These are good grounds to hold that this route though difficult was frequently used

1. Phayre, A.R. *History of Burma*, p.15, 1984.
2. Bullelinde i 'Ecole Francaise De' Extreme Orient, 1904, pp. 142-143.
3. Champa, pp. 13-14
4. Bagchi, P.C., *India and China*, pp. 5, 15.
5. Mc Cosh 'On the various lines of over land, Communication between India and China', *P.R.G.S.*, London, Vol. V, 1860-61 pp. 47-54; Account of the Mountain Tribes on the Extreme N.E.P. Bengal, *J.A. S.B.*, V, pp. 203-204.

I. Gold masked human skull from Lambui Ching Chingmeirong hillock in Imphal town.

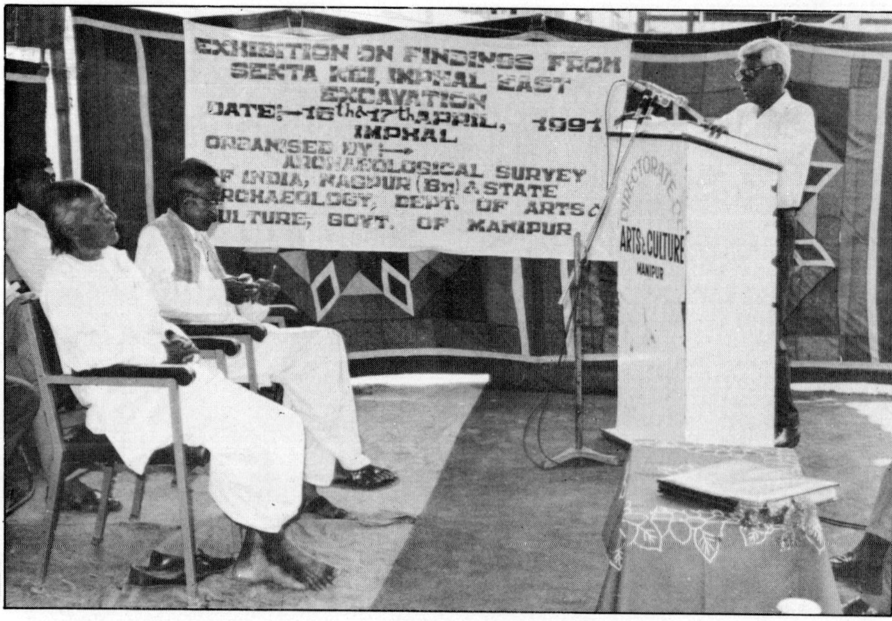

II. A. Seminar on Sekta excavations.

II. B. Students of Manipur University during exploration.

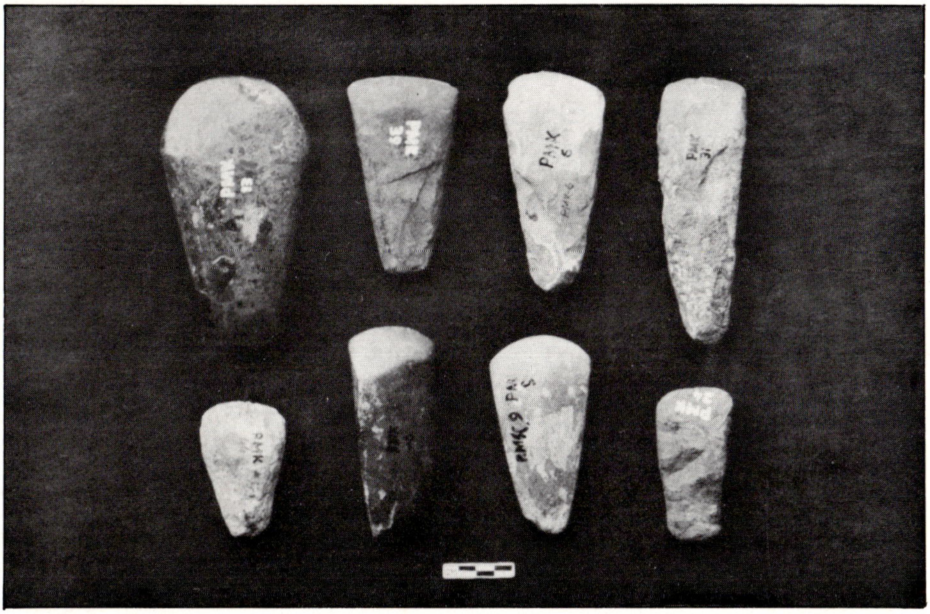

III. A. Neoliths from Manipur.

III. B. Burial jar with antiquities from Pungdongbam.

IV. Emergence of land after drying up of lakes.

V. A. Antiquities from Panjaopalum Ching near Kakching.

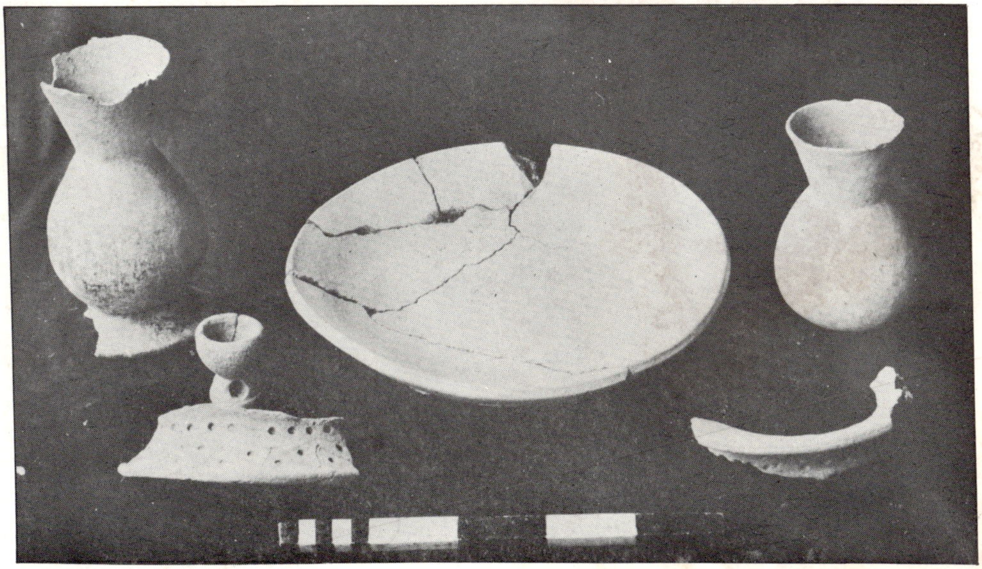

V. B. Antiquities from Panjaopalum Ching near Kakching.

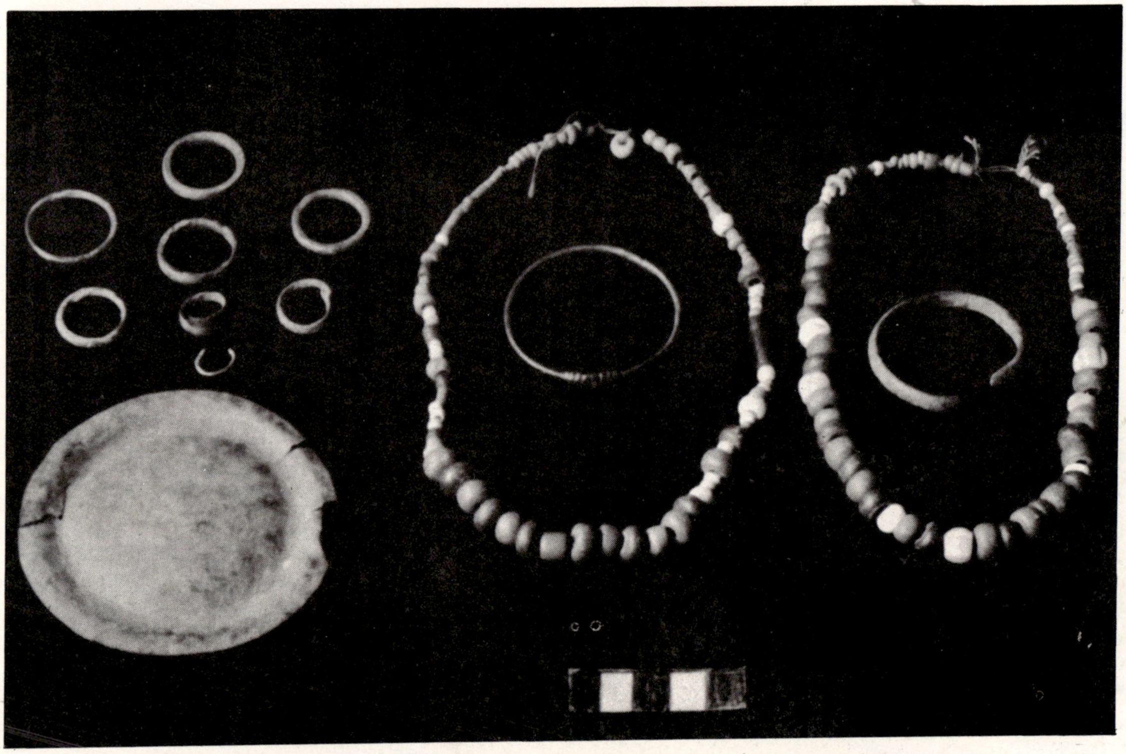

VI. A. Antiquities from Panjaopalum Ching near Kakching.

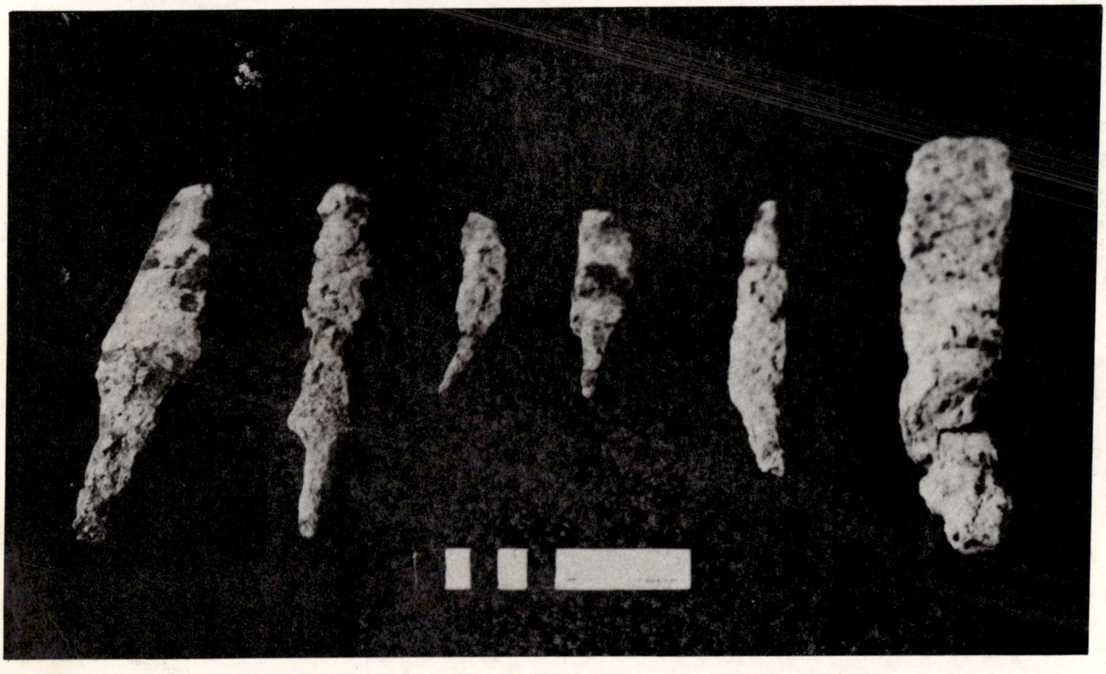

VI. B. Antiquities from Panjaopalum Ching near Kakching.

VII. A. Present Sekta village.

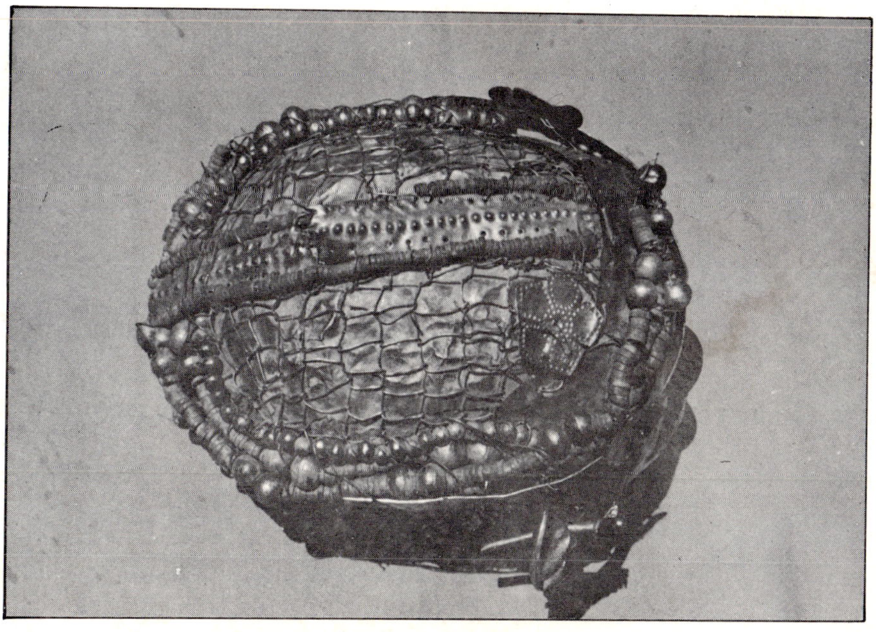

VII. B. Top of gold mask

VIII. Work in progress.

IX. Antiquities from Lambui Ching Chingmeirang.

X. Salangthel menhirs.

XI. A. Findspot of bell metal container.

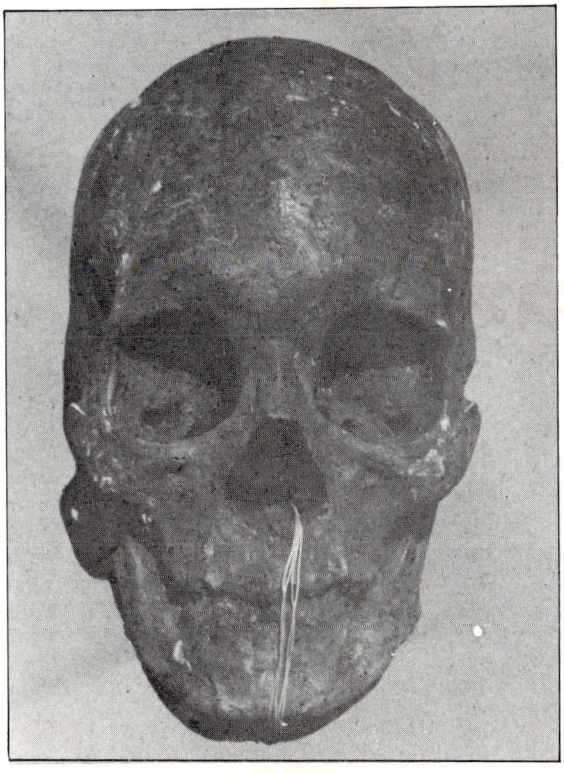

XI. B. Human skull from a hillock near Thumkhong Lairembi, Sekta.

XII. Rock shelter on Thumkhong Ching hill.

XIII. Habitational mound on the slopes of Thumkhong Ching hill.

XIV. A. Stone Anthropomorphic figure on the slopes of Thumkhong Ching hill.

XIV. B. Anthropomorphic figure from Andamans.

XV. The burial mound at Sekta - before excavation.

XVI. Flat alluvial valley sorrounded by hills.

in olden times".[1] G.E. Harvey mentions "Two (routes) were along the Irrawaddy and the Salween rivers, the third down the Chindwin River and through Manipur, for the caravan a three months journey to Afghanistan where the silk of China were exchanged for the gold of Europe."[2] According to a tradition preserved in Burmese chronicle, *Maharaja Vamsa*; one Dhaja Raja, a Sakiyan prince, settled at Manipur about 550 B.C. and later on conquered Tagoung or upper Pagan.[3] The northern part of the Kabo valley which is still called Maurera is said to be the name of the tribe to which Asoka belonged.[4] Pemberton gives a description of four routes, two from India to Manipur and two from Manipur to Burma. These must have been the ancient trade routes."[5]

John F. Cady[6] points out A well-defined overland trade route to India via the Mekong, Salween and Irrawaddy river gorges was opened in A.D. 120. The history of the later Han (Hon Han Shan) records that there was trade between China and India which produced elephants, rhinoceros, tortoise, shell, gold, silver, copper, led and tin.'

Kautilya's *Arthasasthra* refers to the supply of agallochum and sandal-wood from China and her adjoining regions. viz, Indo-China, Malaysia, Timoy, Sumatra and Java through Manipur to India and the Western world. We learn from the classical writers that in the 4th century B.C. Chinese cotton and bamboo were carried through Manipur-Burma route from China to Bactria. It was also through this route that the Chinese silk came to Bharu-Kaccha (Barygaza) which later was imported in the emporia of Seleucia and Alexandria. The kiratas of Indo-Chinese orgin supplied through Manipur to India agallochum, precious stone, sandalwood and aromatics. They also dealt in slaves, rare birds and animals. Chang Kien, a Chinese, was entrusted with the mission in 138 B.C. to proceed as far as Oxus valley (under the Huns in North-west India). He reported to the Chinese Emperor that the commodities of South-west China were being carried by Indian caravans through Burma and Manipur.

'Rudra Yamala' refers to Manipur as a famous pilgrimage centre of India.

THE PEOPLE

Various ethinic groups like the Tibeto-Burmese, the Indo-Aryans and Tai (Shuns) came to Manipur from pre-historic times. The present day Meiteis, the Nagas, the Kuki Chin and other Indian communities are the descendants of the earlier migrants. They are predominantly Mongoloid, with strains of

1. Majumdar, R.C., *Age of Imperial Unity*, Vol. II, p. 652, and *Hindu Colonies in Far East*, p.14.
2. Harvey, G.E., *A history of Burma*, 1926, p.9.
3. Gerini, G.E.R., *Researches into Ptolemy's Geography*, 1968 p.745.
4. Phayre, A.R., *History of Burma*, 1884, pp. 5-6
5. Pemberton, R.B., Report on the Eastern Frontier of British India, 1835.
6. Cady, F. John., *South-East Asia: Its historical development.* 1964

other non-Mongoloid elements. Of the total population of fourteen lakhs the tribal population accounts for approximately 30%. In the geographic classification the State could be divided into a valley in the Centre and the hills surrounding it. The valley is mostly occupied by the Meitei (Meiteileipak) whereas the hills are occupied by the Nagas, Kukis and others. The origin of Meiteis is still surrounded in controversies. Gangmumei Kabui[1] is of the opinion "Thus ethnologically and linguistically the *Meiteis* are Tibeto-Burman Mongoloid with Australoid, Aryan and Thai admixture (including some Negrito and Dravidian elements). Sociologically, *Meiteis* have absorbed these foreign elements and completely integrated in their social structure."

The *Naga* tribes of Manipur consist of the *Tangkhul, Zemei Liangmei* and *Rongmei (Zeliarong), Mao, Maram, Maring, Anal, Moyan, Monsang, Lamgang, Chothe, Purum, Thangal* (Koirao) and *Koireng* who are all chaste Tibeto-Burman speakers. Most of the northern Naga tribes point to Mekhal in north Manipur as a dispersal point, from where they migrated to their present habitat.

The Kuki tribes are a group of *Kuki-chin* family of people. They comprise of 'Thadou', 'Paite', 'Hmar', 'Vaiphei', 'Gangte', 'Simte', Zou, 'Baite', 'Lushai (Mizo), etc. Kuki is a Bangla word meaning hill man. They are included among the *Kiratas*. Though some of the tribes migrated to Manipur in pre-historic times, greater migration took place in 18th cent. A.D.

The Muslims who settled in Manipur during the 17th century and onwards are called 'Pagan'. They had adopted Meitei languages as their mother tongue.

Walter Hamilton a famous English historian prepared a report on Manipur and submitted it to the British Parliament in 1820. He states "Although situated so far to the east, the casseyers (Manipuris) have a softness of countenance more resembling the natures of Hindustan than the Birmans (Burmese), with whom they have very little affinities, either in manners or appearance".

---

1. Kabui, Gangmumei., 1988 'Glimpses of Land and People of Arcient Manipur' in *Manipur Past and Present*, ed. Naorem Sanajaoba, Delhi.

4. The Cuttings

The purpose of excavations at Sekta was twofold: (a) to understand the early history of Manipur in its proper perspective through archaeological evidences as whatever theories and history written so far was based on not very reliable literary and legendary evidences; (b) to fill the void in the archaeological field work in this part of India as not a single systematic archaeological excavation in an early historic and historic site had been undertaken so far in Manipur. Incidently the excavations at Sekta also provided the much needed opportunity to the officers and staff of the State Department of Archaeology and to the students of Manipur University to get field training in an excavation site.

Before the actual dig the mound of operation was thought to contain habitational deposits. Only after exposing nearly 10-15 cms. of the area it became evident that the mound was a burial mound. Essentially only a vertical excavation was envisaged and as such the eastern side of the small domical mound, surrounded by fields and houses on three sides and the river on the fourth, was taken up for digging operations. This being our first excavation in Manipur, we wanted to proceed very carefully, first by determining the extent of cultural deposit and its sequence, before exposing a larger area as, so far, no archaeological time table was available for Manipur, to guide our dig. Right from the highest part of the mound to the eastern part a 10 m X 10 m square was taken up (*Pl.XVIIIA*). Before doing so the entire mound was divided into a 'Grid' so that, in future if we require to extend our area of investigation on any side, we could do so, maintaining, proper link with the first trench. The square was numbered as A1. On the four corners of the square four pegs numbered as A1, B1,XA1 and XB1 were fixed. This system has the advantage of extending the trenches in all the four directions. Though divided for convenience of work and quadrants of one square separated from one another by 0.50m. wide baulks, the entire trench is subsequently treated as one for the purpose of cultural equations by correlating the stratigraphy or layers with each other. Between the two squares a 1.0 m. wide baulk was left. After the dig is over, if need be these baulks could be removed. The square was divided into four quadrants and in each quadrant the area subjected to dig was 4.25 m. each after leaving the baulks of 0.50 m. on all the sides. Thus we had a total of 17.00 sq.m area available for our operation. The trench was laid with the intentions of enlarging the area of operation on all sides, if we got encouraging results and of course if other factors remained favourable. The quadrants were numbered from 1 to 4 in clockwise direction.

Before laying out the trenches, as per archaeological norms, the mound and the surrounding area was photographed in as is where is condition. After seeing the results--we had our own small dark room for developing the films on the site itself--trenches were laid out. Quadrant 1 was first subjected to investigations and Shri.S.Bheigya Singh, Superindentent of Archaeology, Govt. of Manipur, hit the first pickaxe with the cameras clicking (*Pl. XVIIIB*). With the careful dig by the Manipuri patient women under our watchful eyes, and operations through our experienced, seasoned excavation knives, things soon started revealing. With the exposure of the first earthen jar containing fragments of human bones, beads and a few iron and copper objects, it appeared to be a stray deposit. But as we proceeded in the entire quadrant exposing things at the same level at a time, and as a group of pots, containing almost same antiquities were exposed, it became clear that we were digging a burial mound. At this point we reduced our speed and became extra cautious as digging and exposing of burial pots in this humid climate area and that too with a highly sticky dark grey clayey loam having moderate acidic content, and quickly developing cracks on exposure, becomes extremely painful and slow. The uppermost layers contained along with alluvial clay, organic soil of hydromorphic origin also. This organic soil is rich in organic matter and is highly acidic. Due to high percentage of acidity, nitrogen and phosphate, its effect on pots and other antiquities is highly destructive. It is for this reason that in the top layers, i.e. humus and layer 2 we did not get a single intact and full pot. Rims and necks of all the pots were missing and body portion had developed wide cracks (*Pl. XIX*). Of course for this destruction, plough shares of the villagers, who had converted the mound into a field was also partly responsible. After exposing all the burial pots very carefully and treating them with chemicals for hardening so that they do not crumble down, before we had recorded, the entire quadrant was photographed and plotted on a drawing sheet using three dimensional methods. Important antiquities had to be pinpointed on the drawing sheet, closely photographed and carefully numbered. At the end of everyday's dig in the camp (the verandah was converted into sleeping and antiquity cum laboratory room. All the finds were cleaned, numbered, catalogued in antiquity register and packed. Before

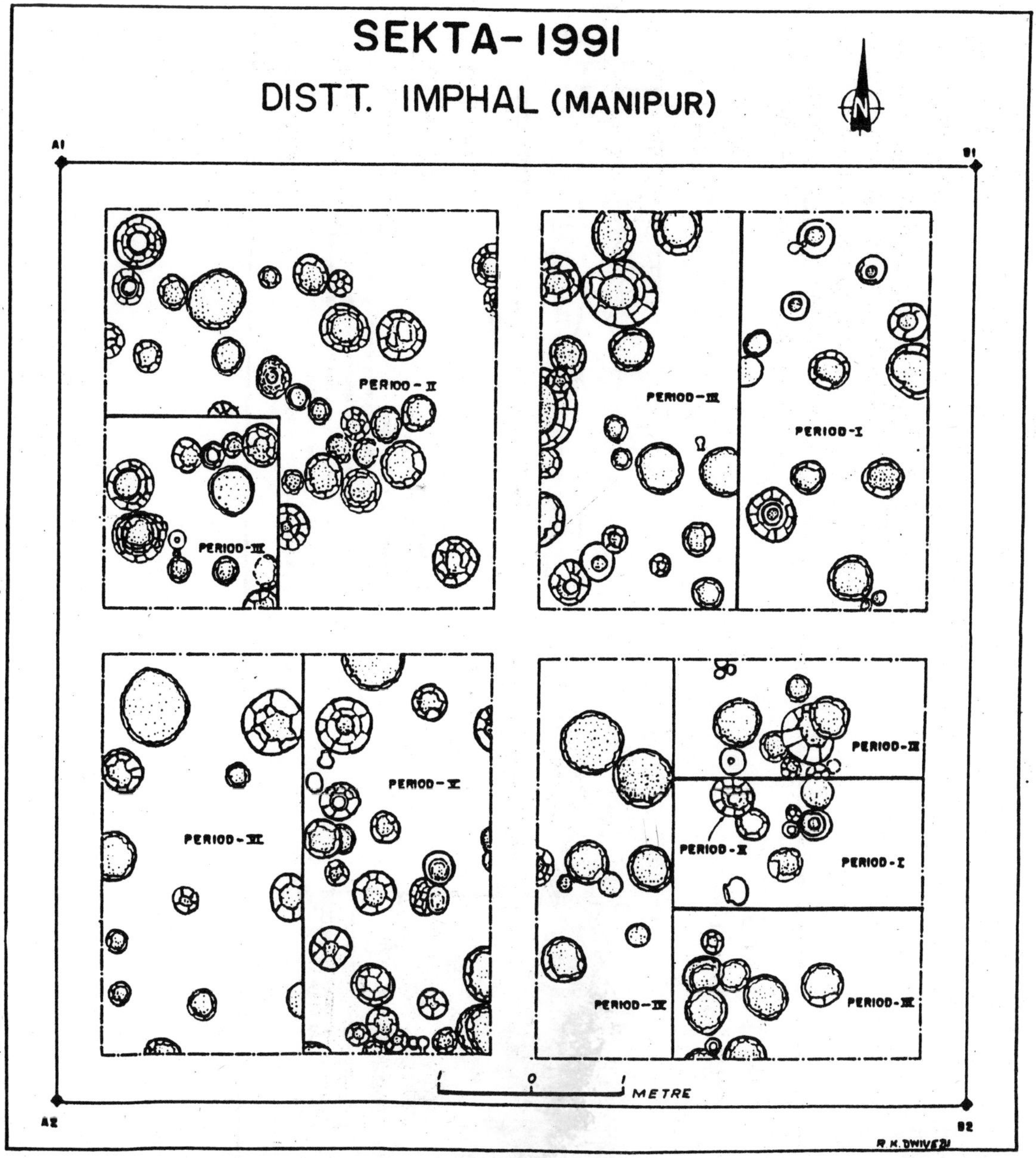
SEKTA-1991
DISTT. IMPHAL (MANIPUR)
N
A1
B1
A2
B2
PERIOD-II
PERIOD-III
PERIOD-III
PERIOD-I
PERIOD-VI
PERIOD-V
PERIOD-III
PERIOD-II
PERIOD-I
PERIOD-IV
PERIOD-III
METRE
R.K. DWIVEDI

Fig. 3

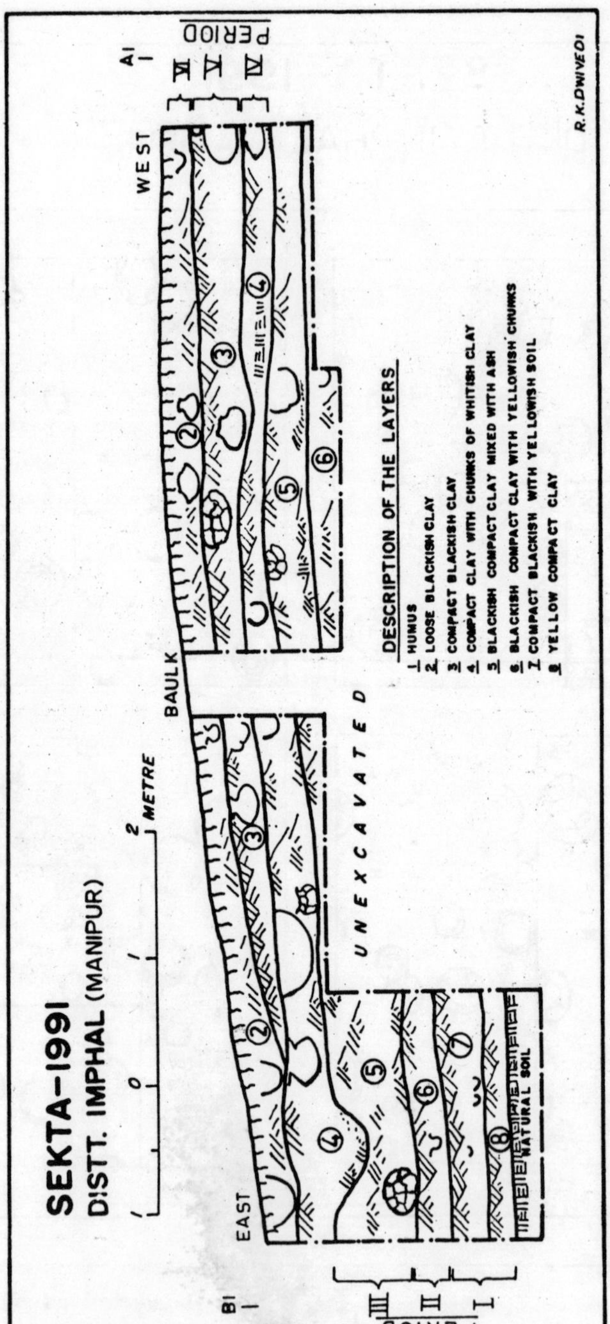
SEKTA-1991
DISTT. IMPHAL (MANIPUR)
1 0 1 2 METRE
EAST
WEST
BAULK
UNEXCAVATED
NATURAL SOIL
PERIOD
I II III
IV V VI
DESCRIPTION OF THE LAYERS
1 HUMUS
2 LOOSE BLACKISH CLAY
3 COMPACT BLACKISH CLAY
4 COMPACT CLAY WITH CHUNKS OF WHITISH CLAY
5 BLACKISH COMPACT CLAY MIXED WITH ASH
6 BLACKISH COMPACT CLAY WITH YELLOWISH CHUNKS
7 COMPACT BLACKISH WITH YELLOWISH SOIL
8 YELLOW COMPACT CLAY
R.K.DWIVEDI

Fig. 4

packing, apart from writing field notes on the spot, detailed notes on each antiquity were jotted down in the field notebooks by the time dinner was ready to be served.

In this fashion all the four quadrants were excavated. After a few days once it became clear that the mound contained sequence of burials belonging to several Periods and once it was decided to preserve the excavated site as a site museum, we had to make changes in our planning. The request to preserve the site as a site museum came from the Superintendent, State Archaeology as this being the first ever excavation of its kind, they were eager to preserve and protect it for the ever eager people of Manipur who by now had started making a bee-line to see for themselves the strange finds of their glorious past coming to light. Quadrantwise we went on leaving the burials Periodwise in different levels so that a complete sequence could be presented to the people and scholars alike. For our purpose also it was ideal as we could in one photograph show all the seven periods of burials in a proper sequence (*Pl. XX*, Fig. 3). Almost each layer comprises of one period as after putting the pots in order to cover them, sufficient quantity of earth, dug up from the nearby area, mostly from the river side, was deposited and as such the layers are homogeneous (Fig. 4). Total absence of any pit or pit lines except in Period I shows that no pits were dug to deposit the burial pots and other antiquities. In the burial ground after performing the necessary rituals, the pots and antiquities were covered up with earth. Normally the skull of the deceased along with other fragmentary bones and offerings consisting of his personal belongings, were interned inside a big jar. In case of Period I, pits have been cut, into the yellowish clayey natural soil, for deposition of burial pots and other grave goods.

Salient Features of the Site

1. The natural soil comprising of yellowish, compact, sticky clay was encountered at the depth of 3.00 m in Quadrants 2 and 4.

2. Above natural soil layer 6 and 7 comprised of dark grey clayey loam mixed with a lot of organic matter. It is highly acidic and contains high percentage of nitrogen and phosphate. This points to growth of plenty of vegetation in the area suggesting plenty of rainfall. Layer 5 upwards, the composition of the soil is compact, sticky blackish clay with slow decrease in percentage of organic contents. This is indicative of the possibility that by middle levels that is around period III upwards process of deforestation of the area had started as people began using more wood for cooking purposes and for erecting houses (*Pl. XXI*).

3. Urn burials of seven Periods were encountered. Due to heavy erosion

of top soil, neck and rim portions of almost all the pots of the available last Period, i.e. Period VII, have been eroded and washed off. (*Pl. XXII*)

4. All the urn-burials of all the Periods are secondary burials where inside the largest urn, human skull, skull fragments, teeth, pieces of long bones and other fragmentary pieces along with other funerary goods were interned. (*Pl. XXIIIA and B*)
5. Each burial has atleast 6 to 7 earthern pots. They comprise mostly of jars, lids, troughs, spouted vessels, bowls, globular vases all in red ware. In almost all cases the centre was occupied by a small black vase. (*Pl. XXIV*)
6. All the interned pots are handmade except in Periods I and II wherein one or two wheel made red ware have also been interned. (*Pl. XXV*)
7. The number of pots interned in each burial shows increasing trend from Period I to Period VII. In Period VI and VII in each burial at least 6 to 7 pots have been interned.
8. In each period groups of pots belonging to one individual have been so kept that they have, normally not disturbed the other burials. (*Pl. XXVI*)
9. Human skulls covered with masks of very thin copper plates were interned inside a big jar. The jar in turn was interned inside another jar of bigger size. Thus there were 3 to 4 pots of increasing size kept inside each other. (*Pl. XXVII*)
10. In case of the biggest jar that contained bones and antiquities, the mouth of the jar has invariably been covered either with an inverted lid or by keeping another smaller globular jar, upside down over the mouth of the biggest jar. (*Pl. XXVIII*)
11. The central vase in each burial is generally always a plain black ware without any designs and decorations and with fine finish.
12. There are pots inside the pot, mostly globular jars and the relics of bones are kept in the central pot.
13. All other red ware, dull red ware and grey ware are hand made, rough and gritty in texture and ill fired. The clay was mixed with quartz, sand grain and stone chips. Most of them had incised and stamped designs of various types described elsewhere.
14. Human skulls were generally found in Periods V, and VI and VII.
15. The antiquities recovered from burials of different periods include iron object, copper and bronze bangles, rings, hollow and solid bracelets, tinklets, flower vases and cups, etc. and a variety of beads shaped

out of terracotta, glass and stones. In some cases bronze vessels and thin bronze plates were also interned.

16. The most important find is a bronze relic casket typical of Buddhist origin from a burial of Period V.[1] (*Pl. XXIXA*)
17. From a burial of Period V a beautiful bronze flower vase was found interned along with the copper masked human skull. (*Pl. XXIXB*)
18. Tinklets were found mostly from Period IV and V. (*Pl. XXX*)
19. Hooka tops of stone and terracotta were recovered from Period III and IV only. (*Pl. XXXI*)
20. Iron objects mostly comprised of knife or dagger, scythe, spearhead, harpoon, etc. (*Pl. XLIII*).
21. Recovery of wheel made pottery, all fine, thin, well fired red ware, from periods I&II only shows that the art of making pottery through the use of wheel was known to the people of Period I and II and later on it was forgotten. This pottery was recovered from the lowest levels of habitation area where a small trench was laid (*Pl. LIV*).
22. From all the three skulls exposed from within the urns, teeth were found to have been removed. This might be connected to some ritual. One skull was that of a child of nearly 10 years of age, whereas other two belonged to middle aged persons. One of the two had three to four cut marks on the right parietal region, probably inflicted with sharp instrument. (*Pl. XXXII*)
23. All the skulls were found to be facing south-west.
24. As the skulls were interned only in few cases and that too with a covering of copper mask, it appears some important persons, or persons from well to do families only had the privilege of this practice, while in case of others only fragmentary bones were interned. Generally teeth have been found whereas in case of other fragmentary parts, mostly pieces of long bones, were recovered in the form of tiny fragments. The condition of fragments recovered indicates that the ritual of secondary internment in pots was done after a considerable gap of time as the bones have almost completely disintegrated. Teeth being stronger have remained better preserved. Incisors and canines were not found.
25. As the pot burials are secondary burials, there must have been sufficient

1. A similar casket made of silver was found in 1980 from Lambui ching, Chingmeirong, Imphal along with a human shull and other gold and silver antiquities which are now housed in the State Museum at Imphal. They were examined by the author in 1990. (*Pl. IX*)

time gap between the primary disposal and secondary one as it will take time for the flesh to decompose. It is not known whether the bodies were exposed in the open or buried and then re-excavated after a lapse of time. The first proposition appears to be more probable.

26. Surprisingly there is total absence of animal bones in the burials, unlike other sites in Indo-Gangetic plains and in South India where animal bones were found to have been deposited in the pot burials. But animal bones were recovered from the small trench taken in the habitation area. The bones contain butchering and skinning marks. The fragments recovered mostly belong to cattle. This indicates that though people of Sekta relished non-vegetarian diet but animal sacrifice did not play any part in the ritualistic practices at the time of secondary internment.

5. Pottery

The ceramic evidence at Sekta, both from burials and habitation, shows cultural continuity throughout right from Period I to VII. In the burial mound there is absolutely no hiatus. The burials continue at the same spot one above other, rather at some places later ones disturbing the preceding ones. Due to continuous use of the same area as burial ground by the people of different periods, there is high concentration of pot burials at the same spot. But broadly it appears from the evidence that people took care not to disturb the earlier ones and as such burial pots of different periods lay divided by the deposition of earth which was done while covering the pots after the rituals.

The predominant type of pottery is handmade, rough ware, right from Period III to the top. Only during Periods I and II we get wheel turned fine red wares, while in period II the percentage of wheel made pottery gets considerably reduced, it is predominant in Period I. This evidence of the burials was corroborated by the evidence from the habitation area, where a small trial trench was laid. It is an enigma as to why the people of Manipur who had the knowledge of making wheel made fine pottery suddenly abandoned this art and took wholly to handmade, rough ware.

The handmade pottery from the burials could be divided into three categories:-

1. Red ware
2. Black ware
3. Grey ware

In all the three types large number of pots are made of impure clay, heavily mixed with quartz and sandstone particles, gritty and ill fired. None of them emits the typical metallic sound of a well levigated well fired pottery. They vary from thick to medium. Most of the hand made pottery is either round or flat bottomed. Pots with pedestal bases are very few which is predominant in case of wheel turned pottery from Period I and II. There is total absence of any painted designs. Decoration is only by employing devices like (i) linear incisions for geometrical and non-geometrical patterns, (ii) depressions of sorts to produce diverse designs and (iii) in few cases particularly towards the later Periods VI and VII, mouldings to produce embossed decorations. A combination of these patterns with ridges or corrugations on the body of the pot, is however, common. In handmade pottery no slip has been applied. Only a single wash was given.

Generally each burial contains a number of pots of different shapes, sizes, and colours. Their number is comparatively less in earlier periods whereas it increases towards later periods. Normally in each burial the assemblage of pottery comprises of a number of big jars with flat bottomed lids kept upside down covering the mouth of the jar, large dish, bowls, basins and vases. There number varied from burial to burial. Smaller pots were generally kept inside the big jars along with other grave goods and in some cases masked human skull. In most of the pots clay used has been mixed either with coarse sand grains or quartz grains to give texture a very rough touch.

Pottery from Period I was mostly wheel turned, thin, fine red ware along with one or two smaller jars and bowls of black and grey ware. Almost all the pottery collected was shaped out of well levigated fine clay having thin fabric and well fired as a result of which they emitted metallic sound. They comprised of small jars, bowls, and vases. Most of them had round pedestaled base.

From the uppermost levels of the trench laid in the habitation area a few pieces of white glazed pottery were also discovered which probably are imports from outside.

Some long necked bulbous jars and spouted vessels, all in red ware, contain stamped designs and symbols. Such vessels are extensively reported from north Indian sites dating from Kushan to Gupta periods. They continue to occur upto the 4th-5th century A.D.

A.Designs

Majority of the handmade pots contain various types of designs on their outer surface. The designs include trellis pattern, oblique lines, diamond shaped notches, straw, reed and cord impressions, fish bone designs, rows of impressed hollow roundels, horizontal thick rows of grooves and sun patterns. These designs occur in red ware, dull red ware and grey ware. Generally such designs and decorative patterns have been reported from Neolithic sites, e.g. Burzahom, Gufkral (both in Jammu and Kashmir), Kuchai (Orissa), Daojali-hading (Assam) and various sites in Garo hills of Meghalaya. Recently during our exploration in Manipur similarly decorated pottery was collected from Laimanai in district Thoubal and from Sachema near Kohima in Nagaland.

The discovery of handmade pottery with above mentioned designs, from the burials at Sekta indicates that the pottery making and designing pattern in Neolithic times was almost similar throughout the country, irrespective of geographical zones and this neolithic tradition while got replaced by wheel made pottery with changes in design patterns in later cultures elsewhere, in

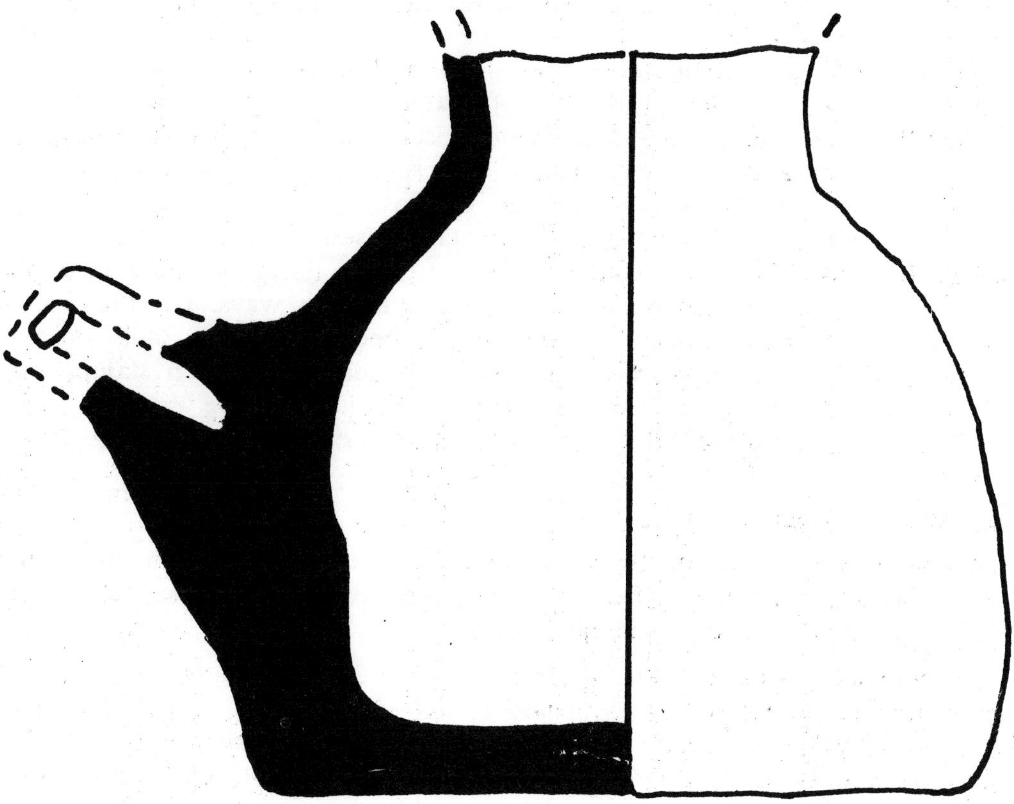

Fig. 5

Manipur the tradition was continued till the earlier centuries of Christian era. This is a unique example of continuity of traditions.

Pl.XXXIV	A	3 - A- trellis pattern, from Period VII. 1 & 2 - Oblique lines in the rim and neck region and in some cases over the body also.
Pl.XXXIV	B	Diamond shaped notches suggesting a honey-comb pattern.
Pl.XXXVI	A	2 & 3 - Haphazard pinched depressions on the neck region while in case of 3 further decorated with oblique incised lines above the depressions.
Pl.XXXVI	B	1 & 4 - Shallow impressed hollow roundels in single file and several rows one above the other. In the space between the rows three wavy lines pass. 3 - Horizontal thick rows of grooves.

4 - Diamond shaped notches along with sun designs in between.

2 - Diamond shaped incised designs with horizontal rows of holes at the tip of diamonds.

Pl.XXXVII A 1 & 6 - Rows of deep incised and raised diamond designs.

2 & 3 - Sun designs almost throughout the body.

4 - Criss-cross incised designs.

5 - Vertical and horizontal incised and raised lines.

Pl.XXXVII B The sun design has been used for luting the base of a pot with the bottom by using it in two ways. On the upper part of base the design has been embossed while on the bottom of the base the same design has been stamped to form depressed design. Just by juxtaposting the embossed and incised designs over each other, a perfect grip has been created.

B.Spouted vessels

Spouted vessels with decorations and without decorations, associated with human burials, are known from Lothal, Rojdi, Brahmagiri, Chandoli, Eran, Inamgaon, Jorwe, Nevasa, Nagarjunakonda, etc.

Ceremonial vessels are known from a few sites from earlier half of the 1st millennium B.C.in North-west Rajasthan and Ganga valley. From about the 5th century B.C. the variety of shapes increased and continued till 5th the century A.D. and even later. From 1st century B.C. to 4th century the occurrence of spouts is widespread.

1. Spouted pot with flaring sides, slightly out-turned, has a flat base and bulbous body. The spout has been made while shaping the body with hand, coarse dull red ware. Handmade from Period VI. SKT 1, A1, Qd.2, (Fig.5).

2. Spouted jar with a bulbous body and long narrow neck tapering into narrow mouth and having circular pedestal base. The long circular, conical spout emerges from one side of the bulbous body and tapers into a narrow channel. It has not been luted but was shaped along with the jar. Dull red ware, fine fabric from Period VI. SKT-1, A-1, Qd.2 (Fig.6)

3. Spouted globular vessel with a very short neck and everted rim and round base. A long tubular spout is emerging from one side at 60^0 angle with the shoulder region which is decorated with horizontal rows of evenly spaced hollow roundels of receding sizes. Space between the two rows of roundels is occupied by a wavy incised line. Base of the body below the foot of spout is decorated with oblique criss-cross incised designs. Coarse red ware without any slip. From Period VII. SKT-1, A1,Qd.4 (Fig. 7)

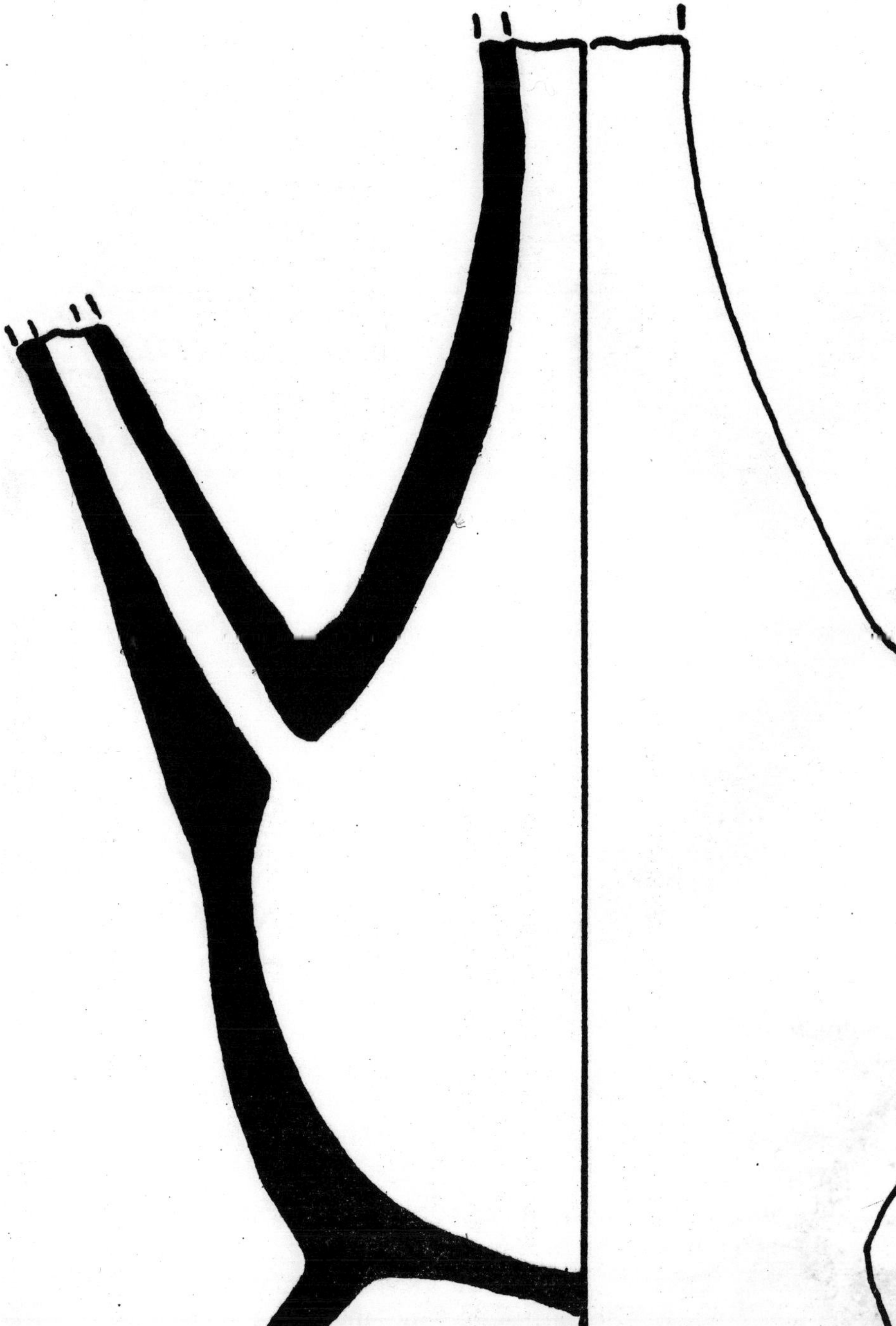

Fig. 6

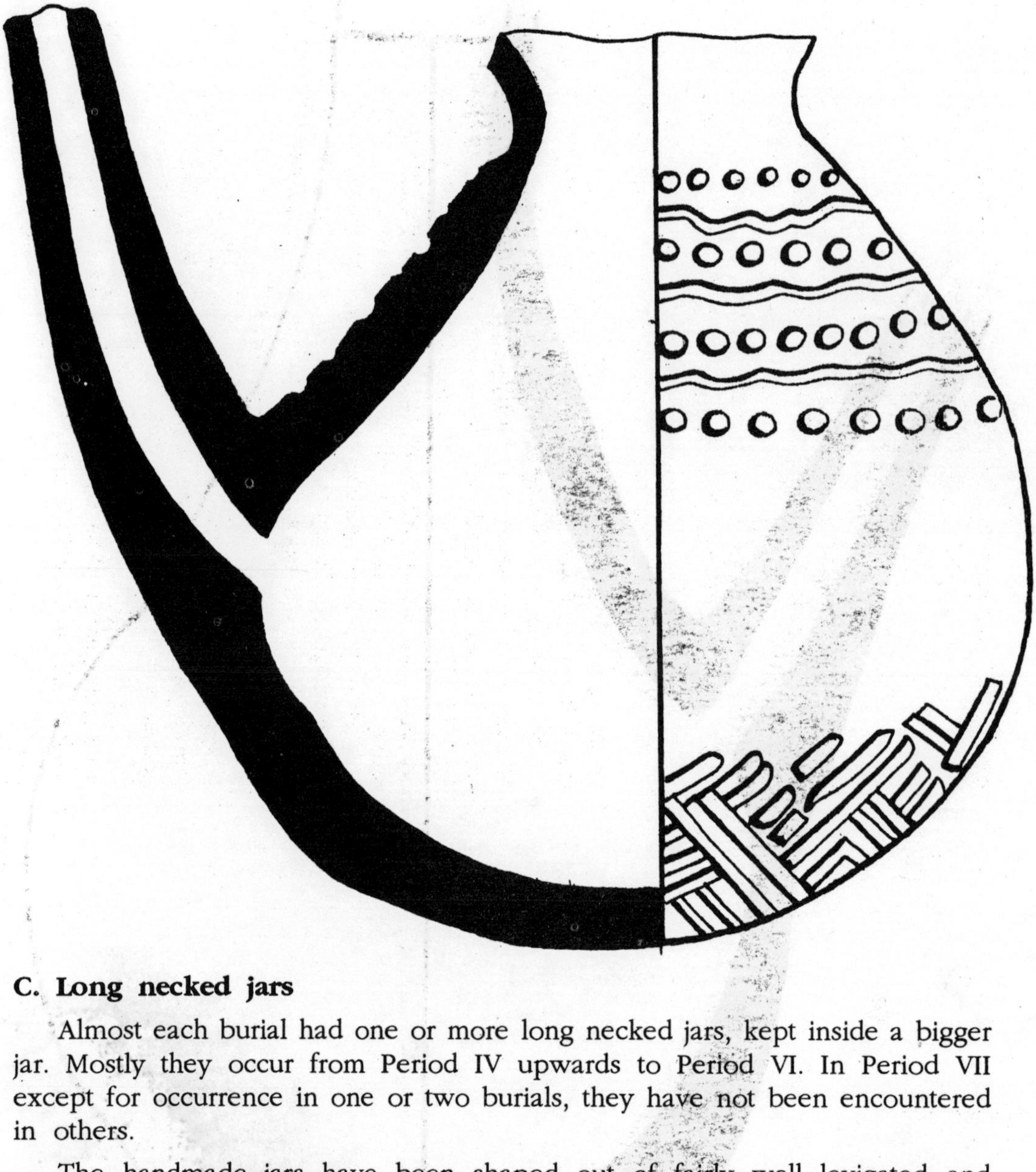

C. Long necked jars

Almost each burial had one or more long necked jars, kept inside a bigger jar. Mostly they occur from Period IV upwards to Period VI. In Period VII except for occurrence in one or two burials, they have not been encountered in others.

The handmade jars have been shaped out of fairly well levigated and elastic clay. Majority of them are in grey colour and a few in very dull red colour. They are with either a slightly convex base or circular pedestal base luted to the main body of the jar. While the interior of these jars is not very smooth, the outer surface has been smoothened by beating with a dabber. None of them has any wash, slip or burnishing. Generally two varieties in

XVII. Remains of a big lake.

XVIII. A. Laying out trenches.

XVIII. B. Hitting the first stroke.

XIX. Soil and burial pots with cracks.

XX. A view of burials of different periods.

XXI. View showing the composition of layers 6 and 7.

XXII. Pot burials from different periods.

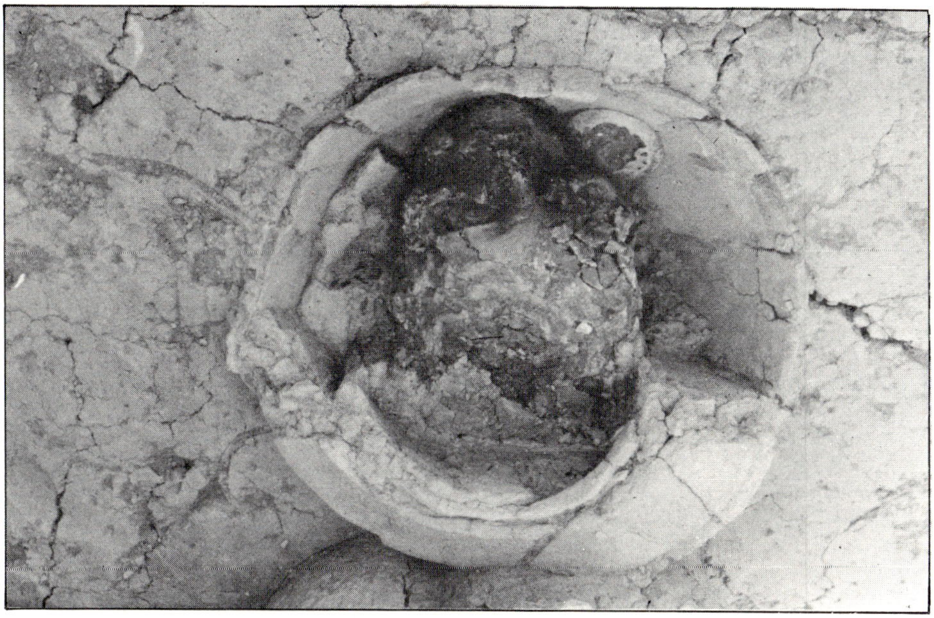

XXIII. A. Urn with masked human skull and base of a bronze vase.

XXIII. B. Urn with antiquities.

XXIV. Close view of a single burial.

different sizes are available -(a) less bulbous flower vase type, (b) profound bulbous, goured shaped body.

4. Almost complete narrow, high necked jar with straight, featureless rim, bulbous body to which is luted a circular pedestal base. Blackish grey in colour from Period VI, SKT-1, A-1, Qd.4 (Fig. 8)

5. A long necked, wide bellied, round bottomed jar, rough in texture, prepared by mixing quartz grains in clay, dull red in colour, rim portion broken. From Period V, SKT-1, A1, Qd.2 (Fig. 9)

6.Medium sized, medium necked jar with bulbous body, flat bottom, slightly outward flaring straight, featureless rim, coarse dull, red colour. From Period V, SKT-1, A1, Qd.2. (Fig. 10)

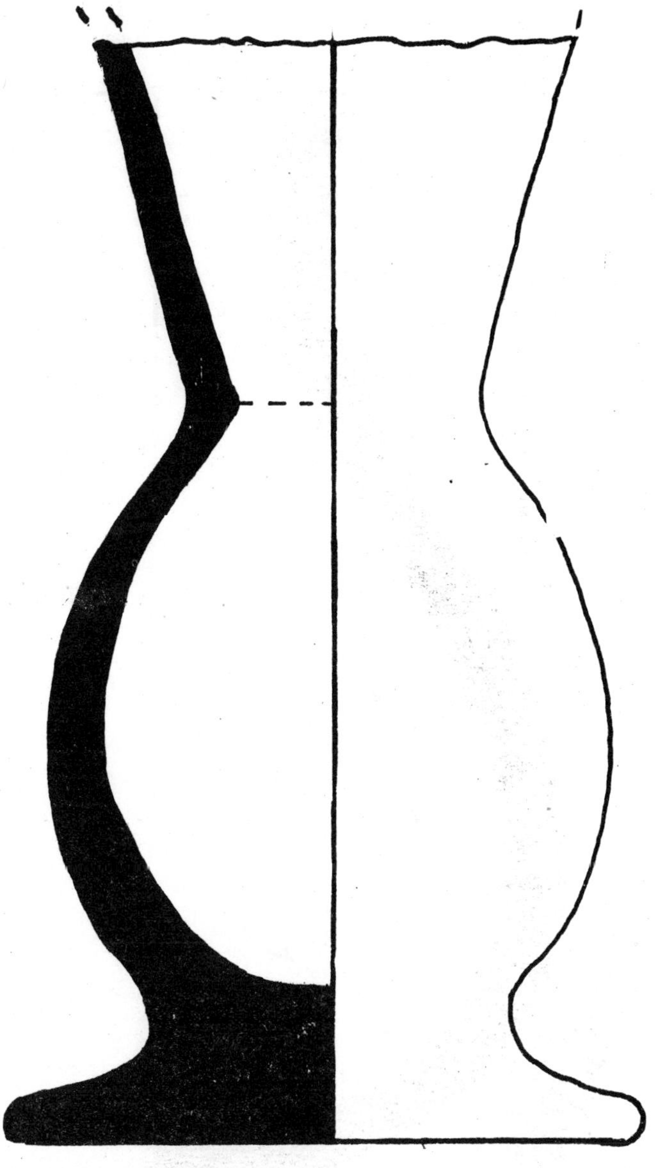

Fig. 8

7. A slightly outward flaring, long necked jar with straight featureless rim, coarse, thick blackish grey ware, slightly convex bottom, wide belly, ill fired, gritty texture. From Period V, SKT-1, A1, Qd.2 (Fig. 11)

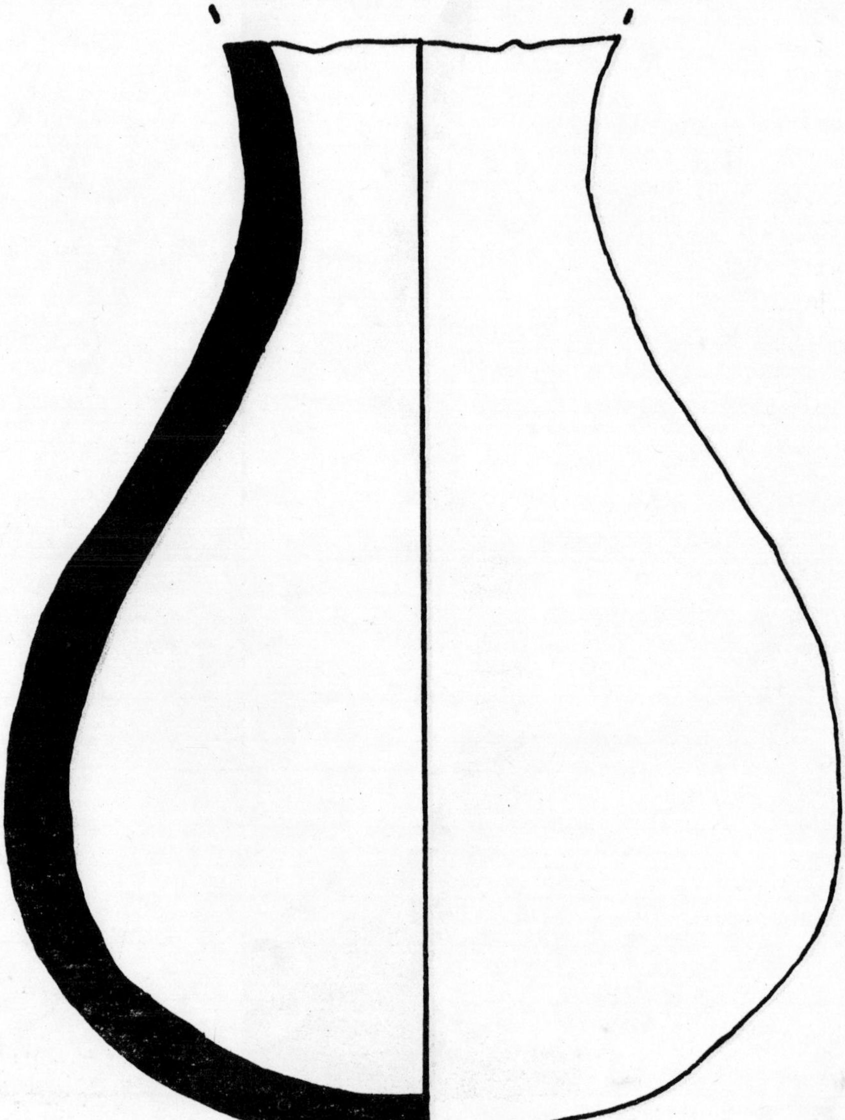

8. A long necked grey ware jar, with featureless straight, thin rim, bulbous body, flat bottom, ill fired, very coarse texture. From Period V, SKT-1, A1, Qd.3 (Fig. 12)

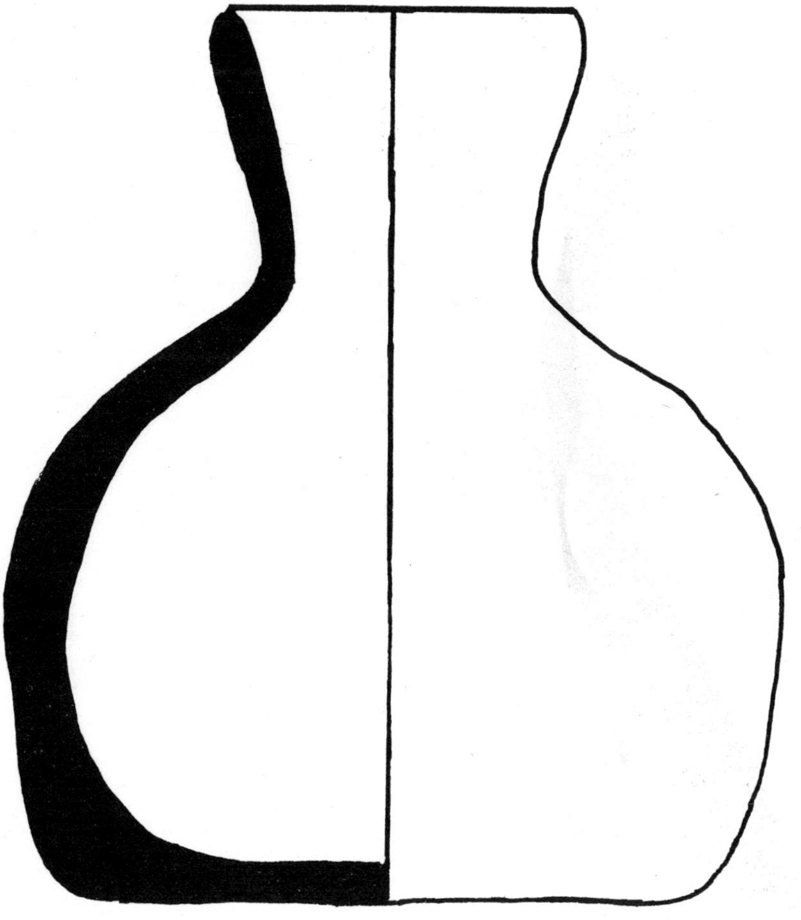

Fig. 10

9. A long jar with outwardly flaring neck with thin featureless rim, slightly bulbous body, resting over a circular pedestal base, moderately thick body, coarse, rough grey ware, clay mixed with coarse sand grains. From Period V, SKT-1, A1, Qd.2 (Fig. 13)

10. A handmade bulbous bodied, long, round, two tiered necked jar with a round pedestal base luted to the body. The neck rises to a height then forms a small bulb and again constricts to end in a very narrow mouth. Such type of narrow mouthed pots are used for keeping oil. The entire bulbous belly is decorated on the upper half with sun designs placed in three horizontal rows. The design has been formed by stamping with a prepared, probably, wooden mould. It consists of two embossed circles with a raised central nucleus

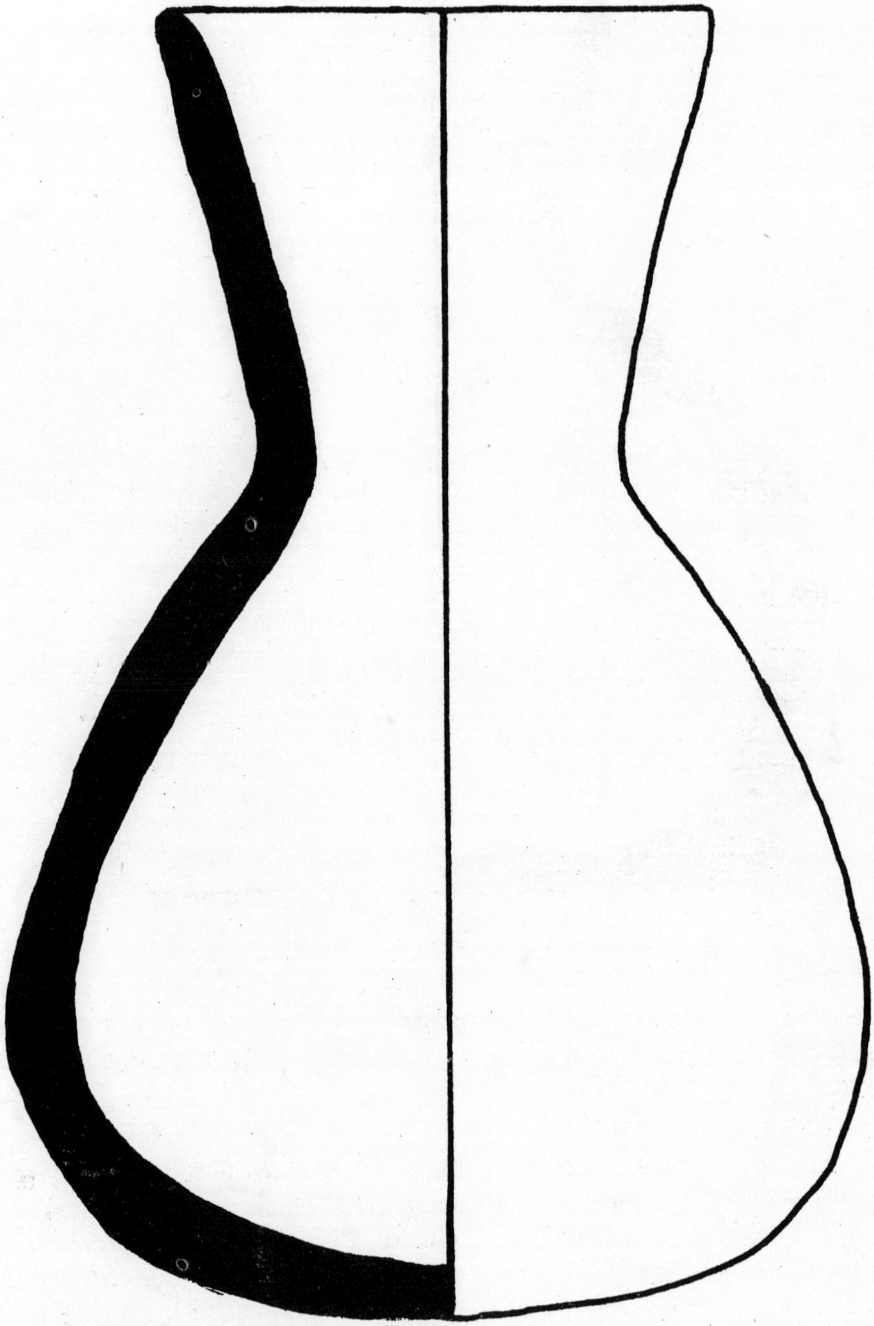

Fig. 11

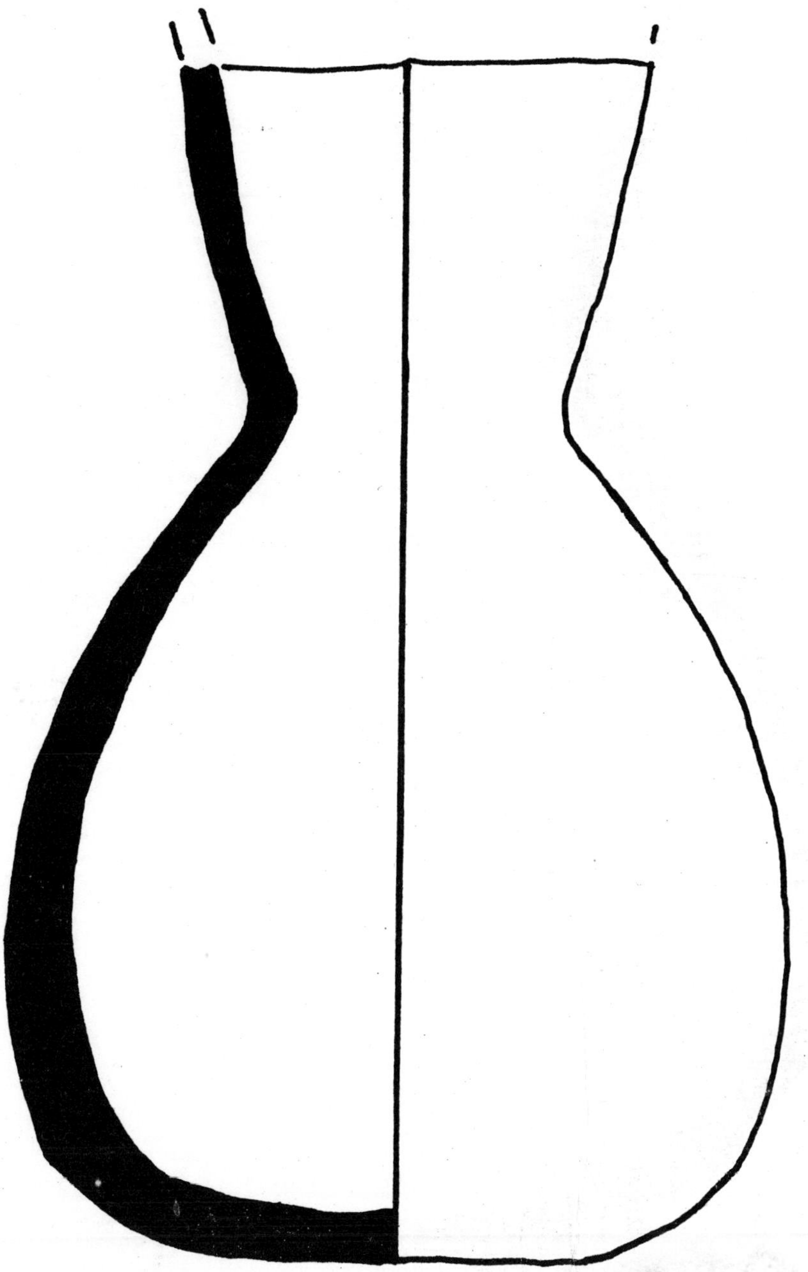

Fig. 12

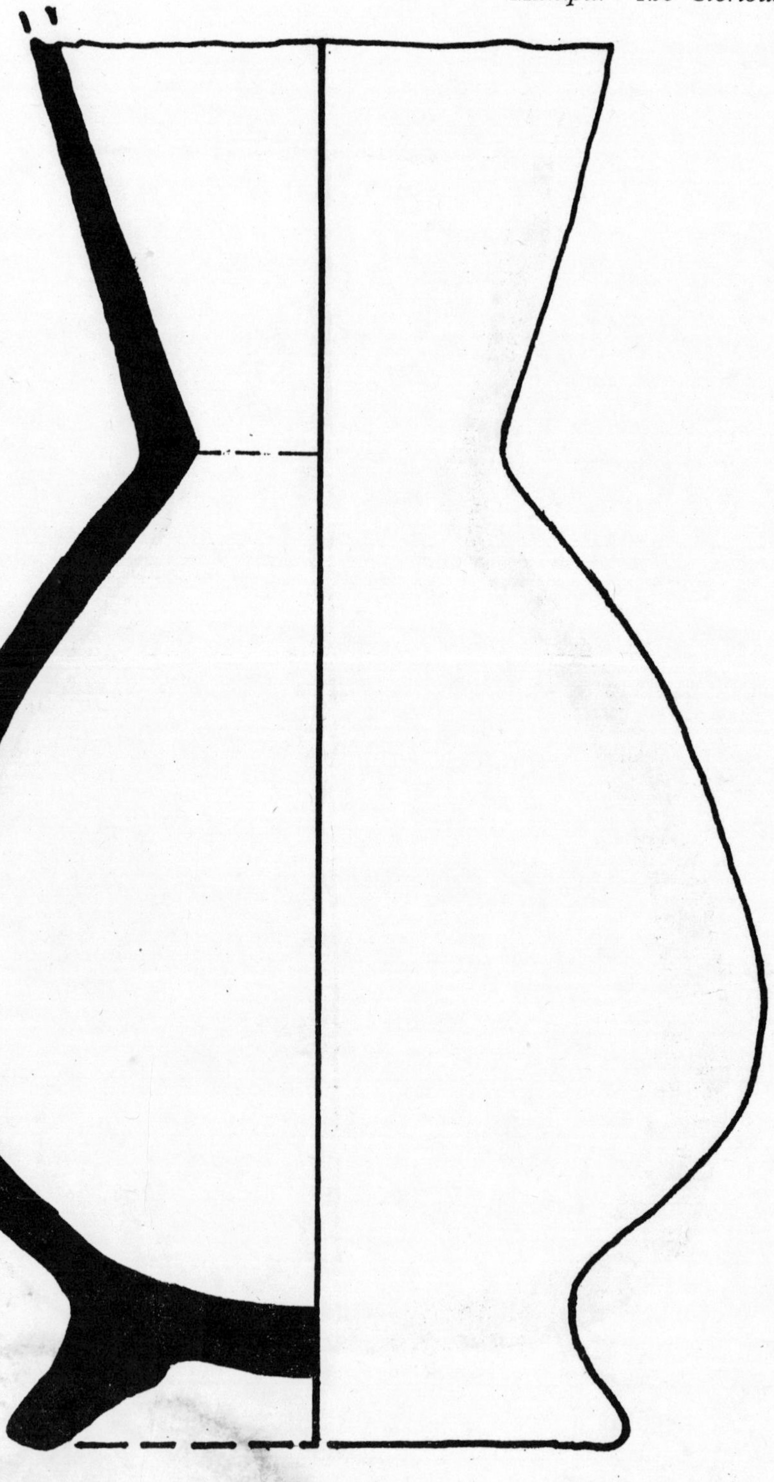

Fig. 13

in the form of a dot. Rays shoot out from the margin of the outer circle in all directions. Lower half has been decorated right upto the point where it is luted to the base, with deeply embossed trellis pattern, forming squares. Fine red ware, thin well fired texture, well levigated clay. Outer side has been given a wash. From Period VI, SKT-1, Qd.1 (Fig. 14)

11. Handmade similar to No.10 with neck portion missing. Slightly smaller in size but made of very well levigated fine clay, well fired, ochre red in colour, with a coat of slip. Almost entire belly decorated with very bold sun designs in three horizontal rows with only the lower margin of belly decorated with trellis design. From Period VI, SKT-1, Qd.1 (Fig. 15)

12. A handmade pot with a globular body, very narrow neck (missing) and properly luted circular pedestal base. Buff ware, rough in texture, no slip or wash is applied, walls are thick, slightly ill fired. Balbous part is decorated with very crude sun designs stamped haphazardly in five horizontal rows. At some part the stamping is deep whereas in other parts it is very shallow. From Period VI, SKT-1, A1, Qd.4 (Fig. 16)

13. A rare shallow based pedestal for a round bottomed big jar. Sides projecting with thin walls ending in featureless rim. Flat base. The central part of base was luted to the outer ring of side walls which is indicated by the presence of a deep circular groove on the outer side of the base. From Period VI, SKT-1, Qd.4. (Fig. 17A)

14. A very rare alabaster basin with a pedestal base from Period IV. White in colour, very fine fabric. From the entire dig only one pot of this variety was recovered from inside a big jar containing other funeral goods like beads, fagmentary bones, etc. SKT-1, Qd.2. (Fig 17B)

D.Troughs

15. A large shallow trough with carinated hollow pedestal base. Above and below the carination is decorated with a horizontal row of hollow roundels each. A deep groove runs round on top of the rim, inner side of which is decorated with a single row of shallow roundels. Sides tapering. Red ware of coarse gritty fabric without slip, clay mixed with quartz grains, inner side blackish. Ill fired, handmade. From Period VII, SKT-1, A1, Qd.2 (Fig. 18-7)

16. A large shallow thick walled trough with straight sides and flat rim. Coarse gritty fabric; clay is mixed with grains of sand and chips of stone. Ill fired, handmade, buff ware, Outer side of rim and neck region are decorated with oblique and crisscross incised lines. From Period IV, SKT-1, A1, Qd.3 (Fig. 18-11)

17. Similar to no.16, except for the difference that in this case inner the

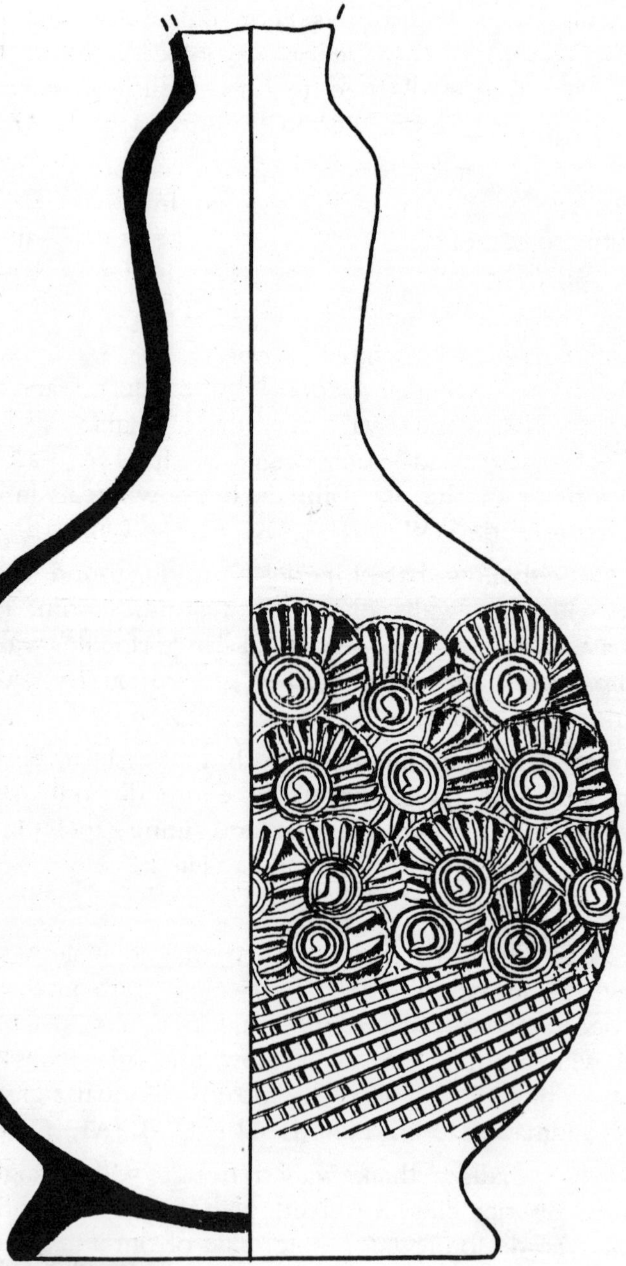

Fig. 14

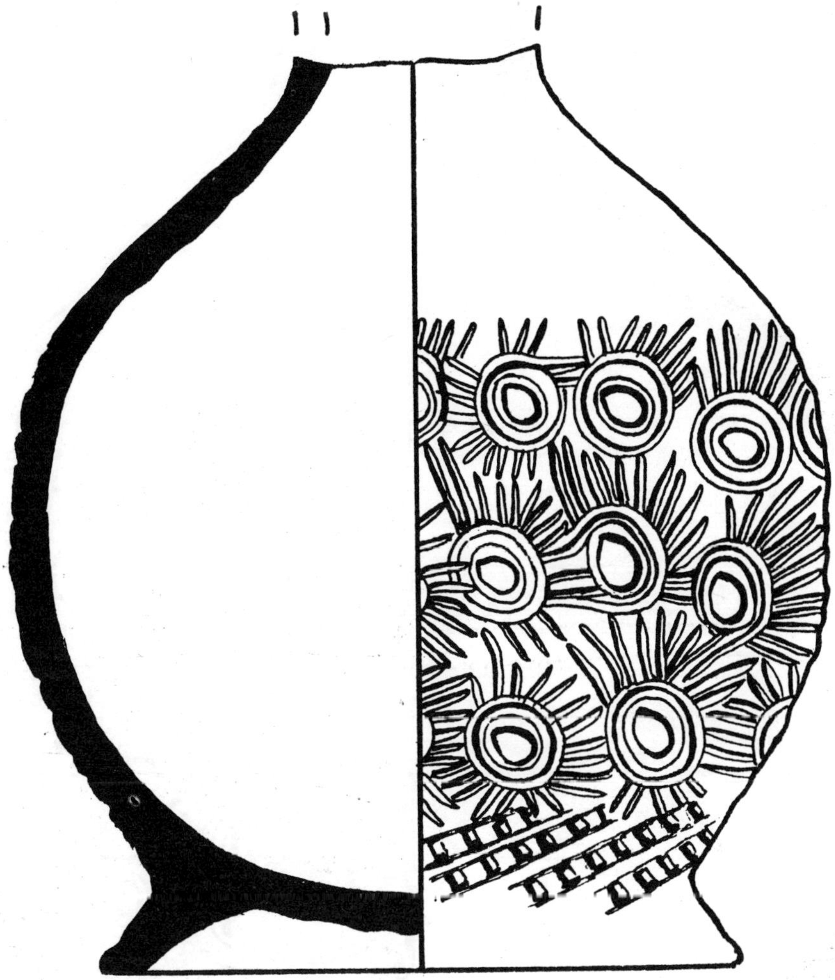

Fig. 15

side is black while the outer side is buff. Shallow flat bottomed trough from Period VI.SKT-1, A-1, Qd.3. (Fig 19-19)

18. Similar to No.17, but is smaller in size. Flat rim has a slight carinated projection outwards and another carination at the junction of sides and base. Buff, coarse gritty ware with plenty of sand grains mixed with clay. Ill fired, From Period V, SKT-1, Qd.2. (Fig. 18-12)

19. A shallow trough similar to No.18, but is inner side is black and outer

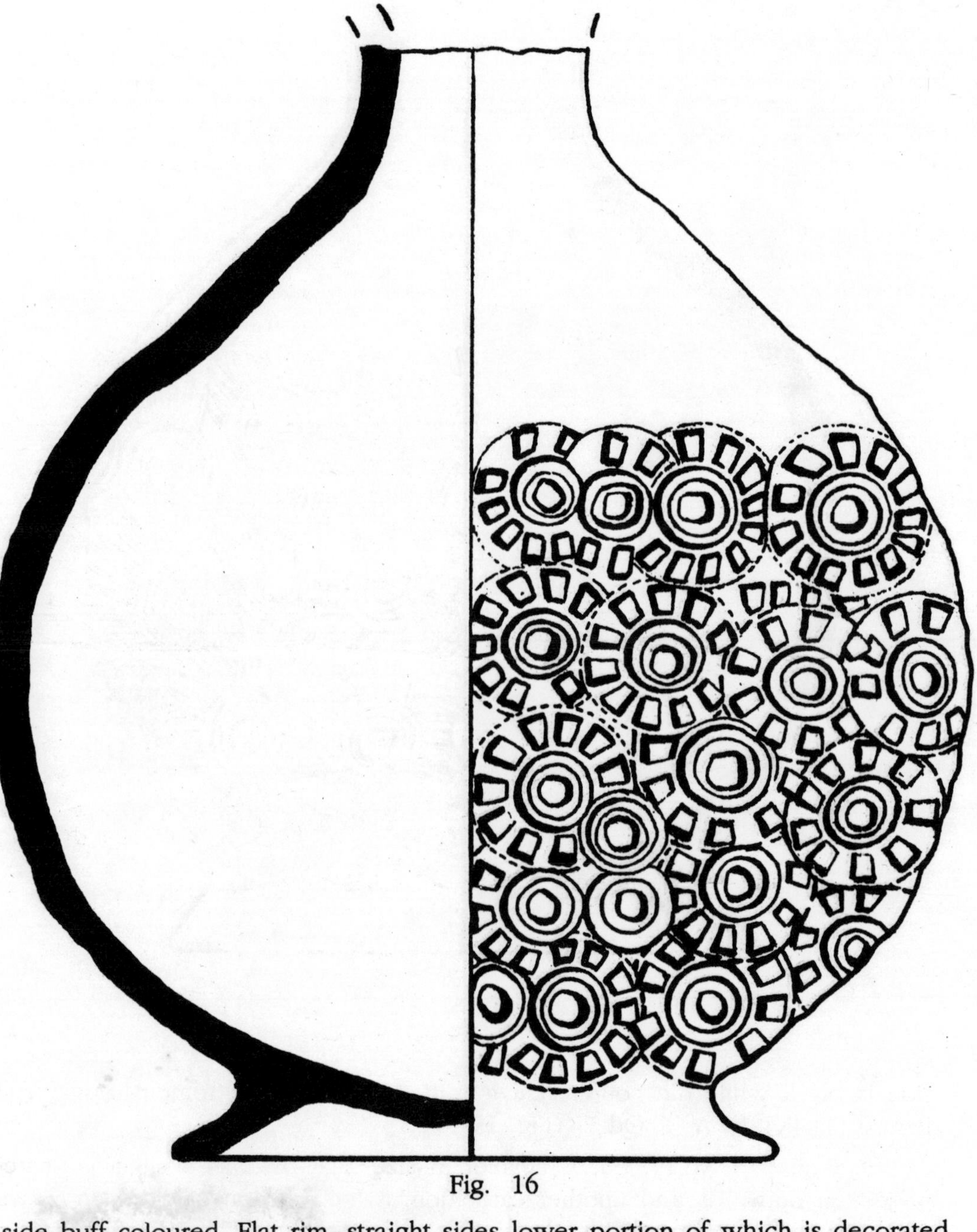

Fig. 16

side buff coloured. Flat rim, straight sides lower portion of which is decorated with a row of oblique incised thick lines. From period VI. SKT-1, A1, Qd.3.

20. A large shallow trough in red ware, outer straight sides are plain with only a horizontal deep groove below the neck religion. Inner side is decorated

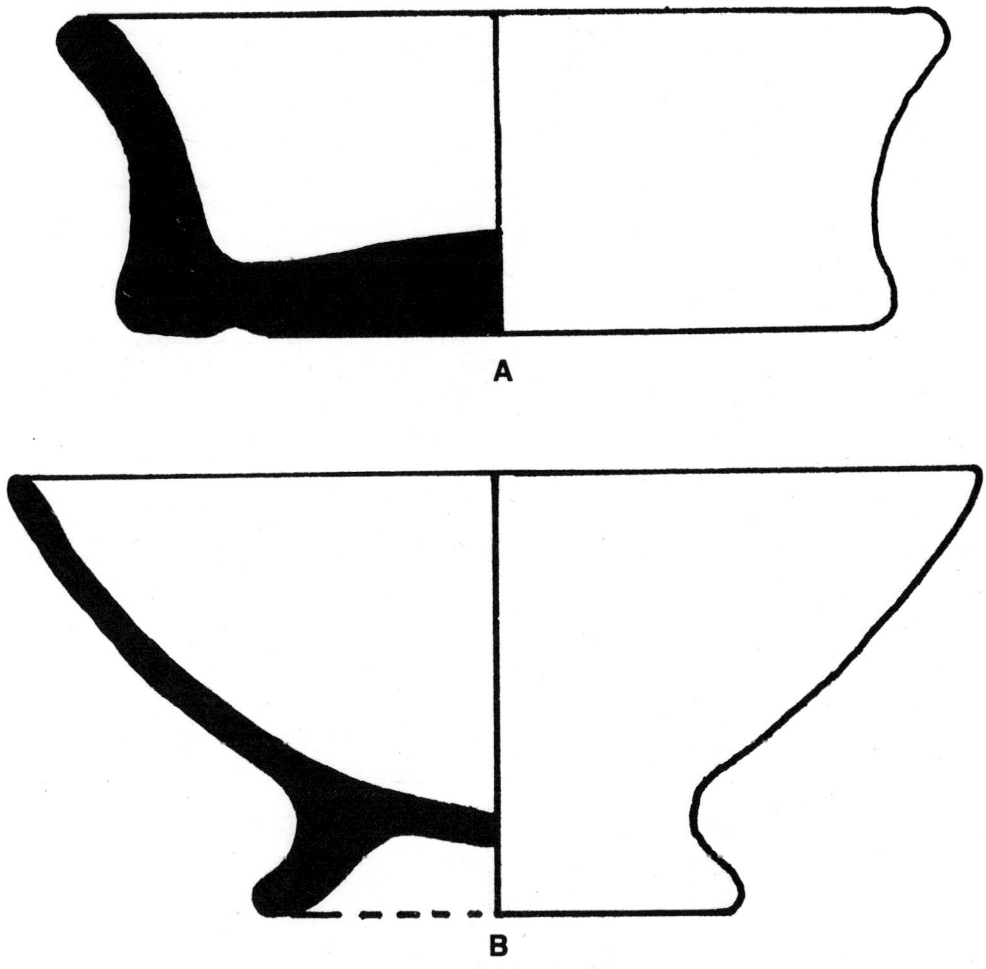

Fig. 17

with deep, hollow roundels upto the out curved and grooved rim. In the neck region amongst the roundels runs a deep incised double wavy line. Of coarse fabric, ill fired and treated with slip. From Period IV, SKT-1, A1, Qd.2. (Fig. 19-1)

21. Another straight sided small trough in grey ware with outer side and flat rim which is projecting inwards and outwards, decorated with horizontal rows of deep roundels having three deeply grooved wavy lines. Coarse fabric. From Period IV. SKt-1, A-1, Qd.3 (Fig. 18-2).

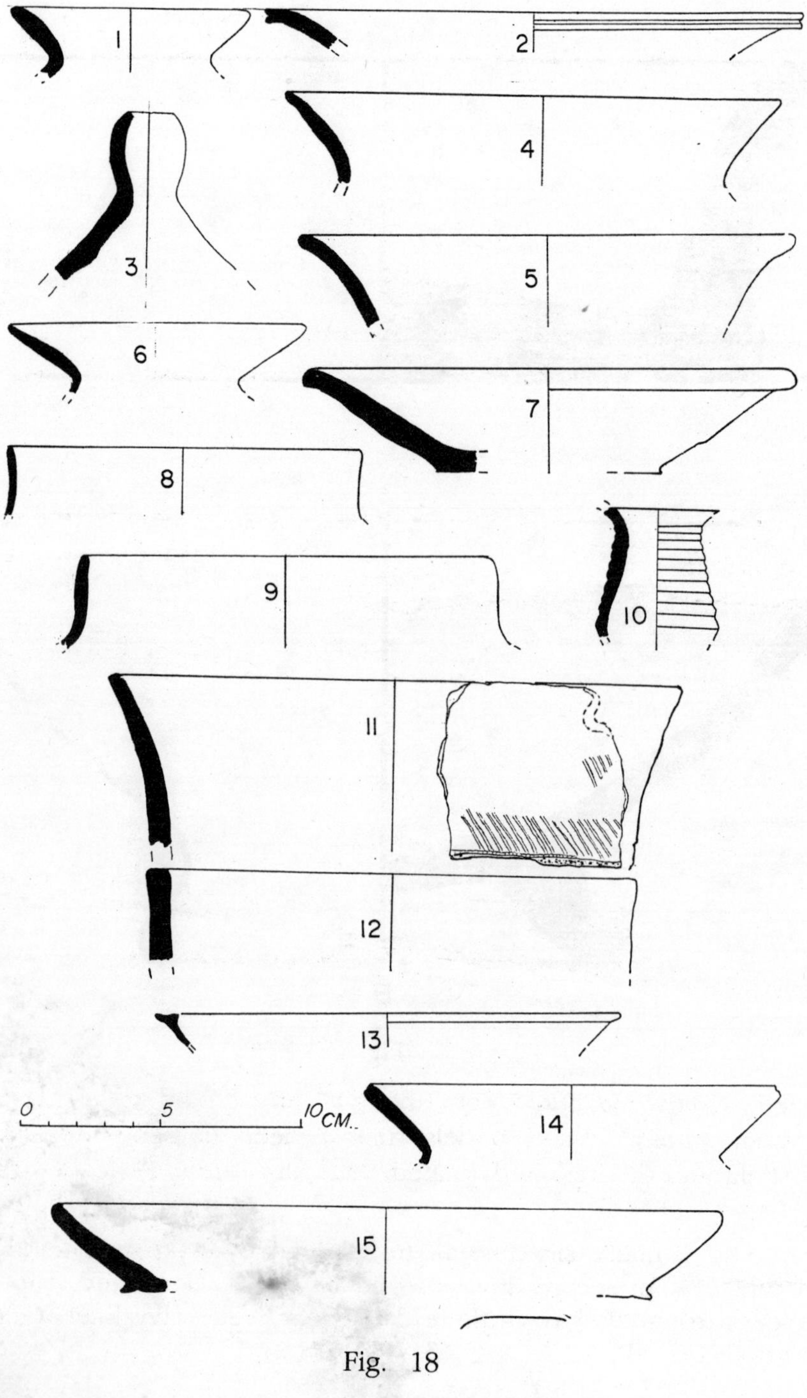

Fig. 18

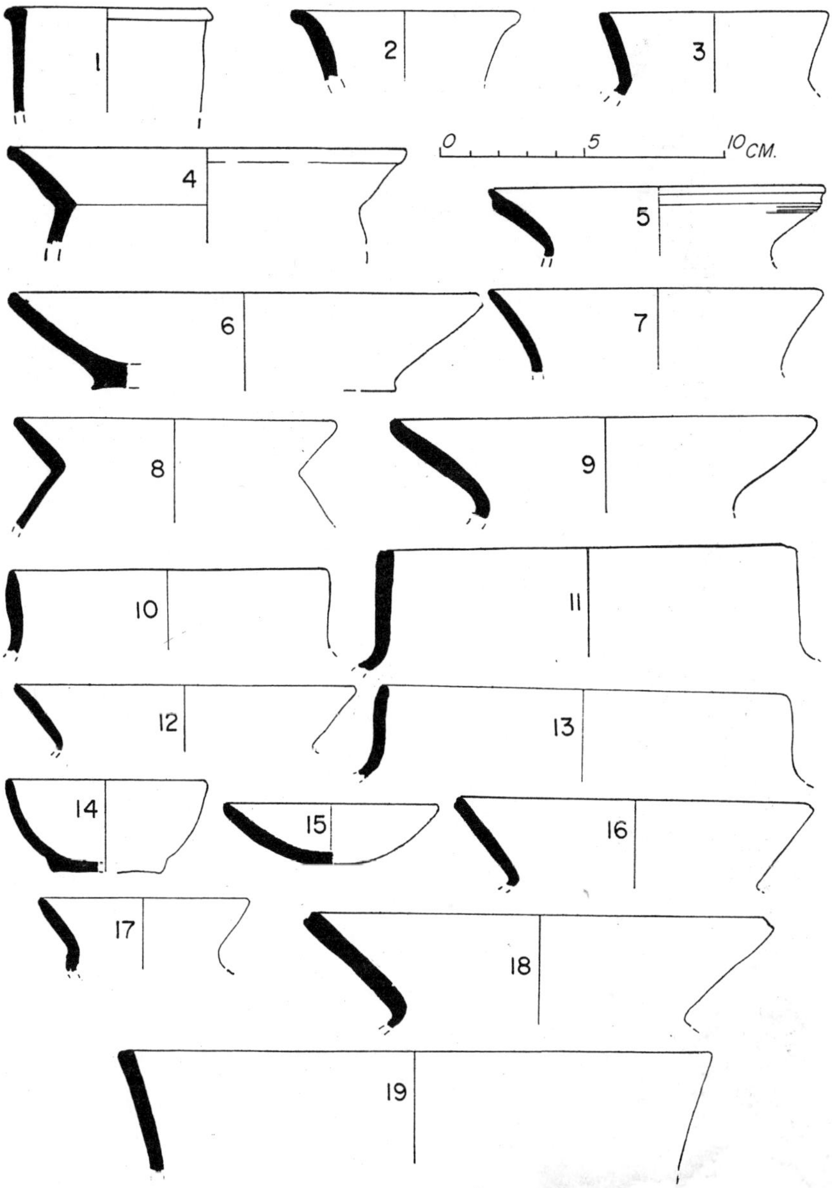

Fig. 19

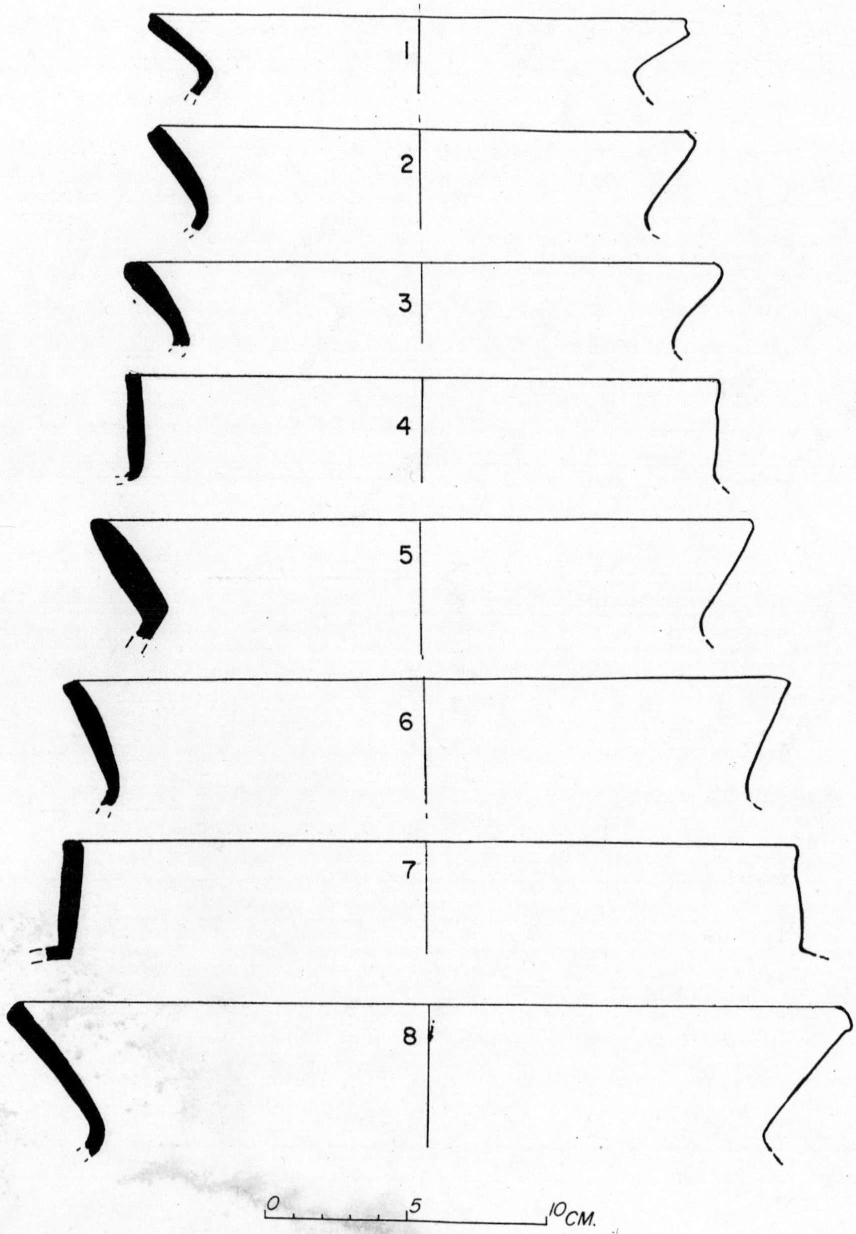

Fig. 20

E. Bowls

22. Medium sized bowl in red fabric with outcurved flaring rim and extending sides of thin section. Outer side below neck region is decorated with large trellis pattern running horizontally. From Period VII, SKT-1, A1, Qd.2. (Fig. 19-6)

23. Piece of a vessel with a straight neck and concave rim, sides expanding to form a bulbous body. Dull red warė with coarse fabric. From Period IV, SKT-1, A1, Qd.3. (Fig. 19-11)

24. Piece of a bulbous bowl in coarse grey ware with a narrow high neck curling out concave rim and expanding sides. Portion below neck region is decorated with stamped sun designs. From Period IV, SKT-1, A1, Qd.2. (Fig. 19-18)

25. Fragment of a bowl with rounded rim and saggering base, of gritty dull red ware, blackish outside which is decorated with rows of shallow roundels. From Period VII, SKT-1, A1, Qd. 2. (Fig. 19-15)

F. Jars

26. Piece of a handmade big jar with straight neck and flat rim, gritty buff ware, ill fired. Outside is decorated with a row of oblique incised lines alternately forming ridges and furrows. From Period III, SKT-1, A1, Qd.2. (Fig. 22-7)

27. Similar as above but in red ware with rim having a deep groove. Coarse gritty fabric with plenty of sand grains mixed with clay. Outside available neck region is decorated with deep holes. From Period VII, SKT-1, A1, Qd.4 (Fig.20-4)

28. Piece of a jar with straight neck and corrugated rim, in red ware, coarse fabric; outside near the rim decorated with oblique deep groove. From Period VI, SKT-1, A1, Qd.2. (Fig. 18-9)

29. Piece of a large pot with straight, slightly flaring neck and flat rim with a deep furrow. Buff, gritty, rough ware, with vermilion coloured slip applied inside and decorated with incised large diamond designs inside of which are a few pinched hollow, shallow roundels. From Period VII, SKT-1, A1, Qd.1. (Fig. 18-8)

30. Piece of a small shallow bowl, in dull coarse cream ware. Rim carinated on inner side and outer side is slightly projecting. From period V, SKT-1, A1, Qd.3. (Fig. 18-13)

G. Wheel made pottery from habitation

Pottery recovered from the lower levels of a small slit cut in the field in the habitation area predominantly comprises of very fine thin and slightly thick red ware all made on wheel. They mostly comprise of small bulbous bowls with circular pedestal base. They have been made out of very fine well levigated clay, devoid of any impurities and air bubbles and have been well fired giving uniform colour to the fabric of the pot. Doubts were raised by some scholars regarding their being wheel made, but the fine shape and wheel marks in the form of perfect circular striations on inner and outer surfaces and on the bottom of the base are clear and firm evidences of their being wheel made. Similar wheel made pottery has come from Period I and II of the burials. As only a limited area of these periods was exposed and as it was decided to conserve them in situ for a site museum, they were not lifted, hence not described here specimen wise.. The wheel made pottery has been treated with fine slip.

31. Piece of a medium sized *lota*-shaped vessel with a short neck and everted round rim. Clay is well levigated and fired creating a uniform fabric, slip applied. Though the base is not present but other pieces recovered indicate that it was having a circular pedestal base.

32. A globular miniature vessel, probably with a flat bottom, having a short flaring rim with flat top. Its fabric is finely levigated red clay. Wheel marks are clearly visible.

33. A miniature vessel of very fine levigated red clay with thin uniform fabric treated with red slip on the exterior; it has an out-curved and flanged rim. Wheel made.

34. Similar to 33 but smaller in size. Slip applied both internally and externally. Striation marks on inner face clearly visible.

35. Jar of red ware, medium fabric treated with slip on both the sides, having an externally thickened rim and a splayed tall neck. A similar shape occurs at Hastinapur [1] and Nagada. Well levigated clay, fine fabric.

36. A variant of 35 in red ware. Similar shape also occurs at Sravasti.[2]

37. A small basin of red ware, has a incurved flat rim, and of fine fabric.

H. Bases

38. Circular pedestal base of a vase or goblet of red ware, medium fabric, treated with slip. In the bottom of the base wheel marks could be clearly seen.

---

1. *Ancient India*, Nos. 10 & 11 p. 60, fig. 18; 32
2. *Indian Archaeology 1958-59- A Review*, p. 49, fig. 22; 20.

XXV. Wheel made pots in Period I and II.

XXVI. Pot burials from different periods.

XXVII. Human skull with copper mask in a jar inside another jar.

XXVIII. Mouth of jar covered with an inverted lid.

XXIX. A. Bronze relic casket.

XXIX. B. Bronze vase with copper masked skull.

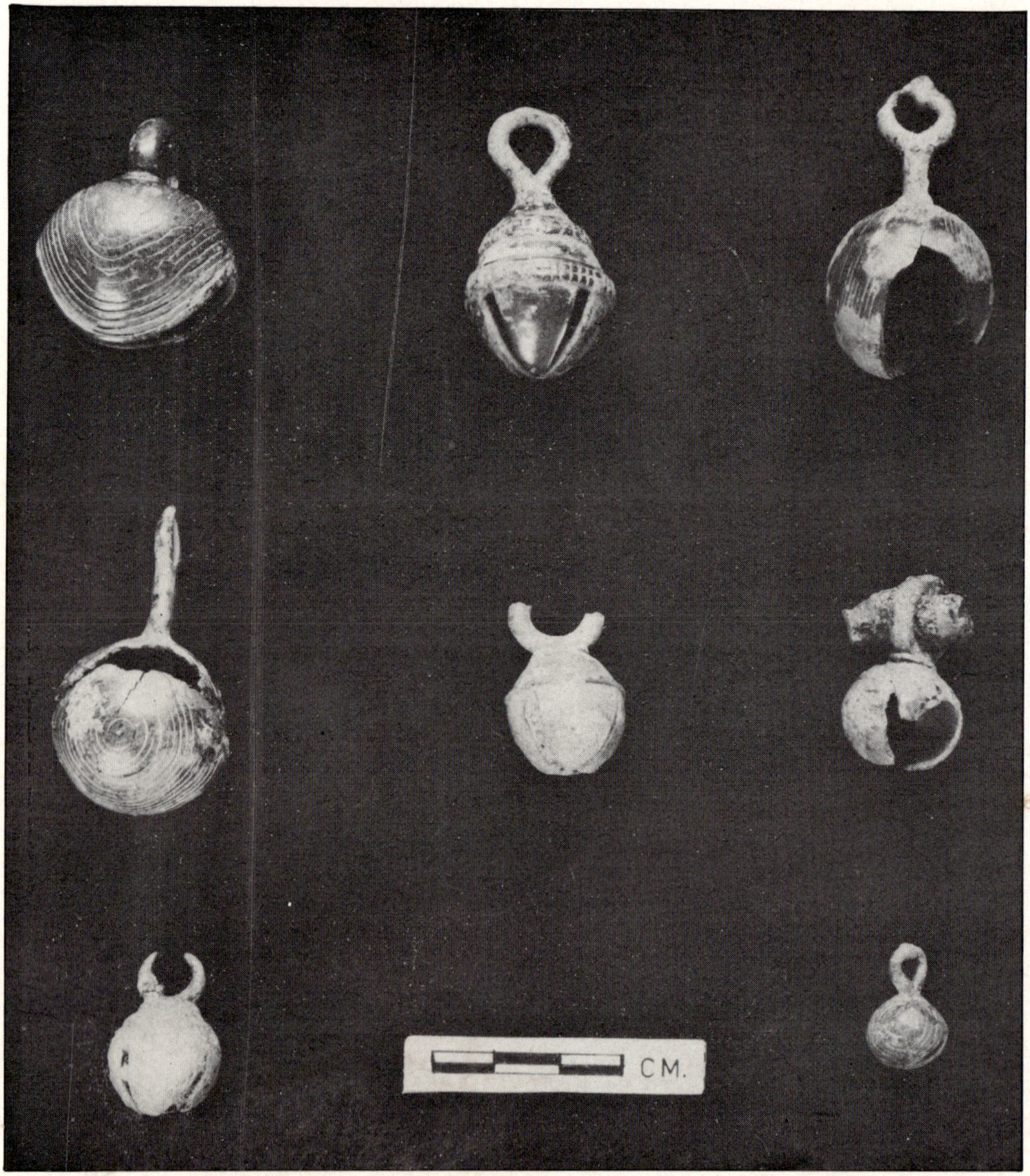

XXX. Bronze Tinklets.

XXXI. Hooka tops.

XXXII. Copper masked human skull.

XXXIII. Bulbous jars and spouted vessels.

XXXIV. Designs in pottery.

XXXV. Designs in pottery.

XXXVI. Designs in pottery.

XXXVII. Designs in pottery.

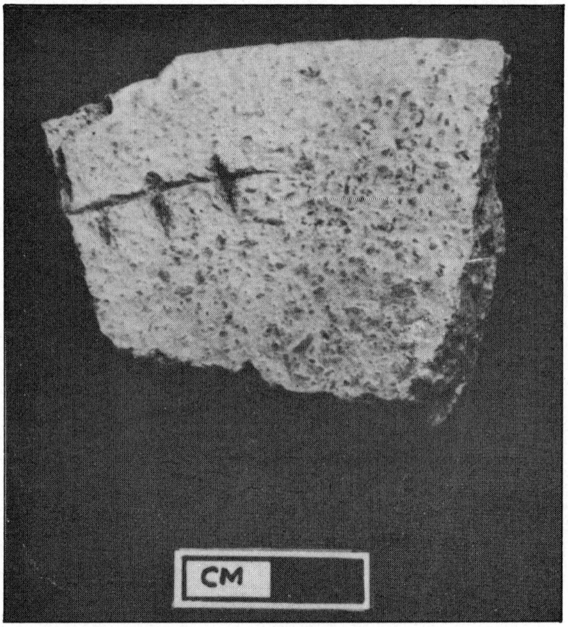

XXXVIII. A. An incised scale.

XXXVIII. B. Iron spearhead in-situ.

XXXIX. Iron objects.

XL. Iron objects.

39. A variant of 38 of red ware, fine fabric with a better slip.

40. Circular pedestal base of red ware, very fine fabric, well levigated clay, well fired, emitting metallic sound. Wheel marks are more pronounced on the inner side of the base.

41. A variant of 40, but of very fine thin fabric, red ware., circular pedestal base thin and flaring rim.

From the trench in habitation area two terracotta legs of different sizes of legged vessels were recovered. Such legged vessels have been often found by villagers while ploughing in the field or digging for foundation of houses.

6. Other Goods from the Burials

A. Hooka tops

Five hooka tops (in which tobacco and fire are kept) were recovered from the burials. One was collected from the surface. They occurred right from Period III to VI. Four of the tops are made of terracotta whereas the remaining two are of sandstone. Except one all are flat bottomed. The lone specimen has a rounded convex bottom. Four of the specimens are having holes on the side for attachment of pipe whereas the other two have no side holes and were thus attached directly to the hooka. This indicates that two types of hookas were in use-- i) where smoke used to be sucked directly from the ignited tobacco and ii) where the smoke will first pass through water and then to the smoker through a pipe attached to a separate water pot. The second one is a more advanced type.

No.1 SKT-91, Location A1, Qd.3, A-2 - 7.45 m. B2 - 2.65 m. depth 0.75, layer 5, Period III. Made of terracotta, well levigated fine clay, ill baked, flat bottomed. The hole for insertion of the pipe is located on the solid pedestal just below the constricted joining point with the cup shaped top. Tobacco and fire container portion is having straight featureless rim; the outer surface of this part is decorated with four horizontal grooves of equal thickness, whereas the inner surfaces show soot and use marks. The hole in the bottom of the upper part leads to the hole on the pedestal. Handmade. Total height 5.20 cm, height of the fire pot 2.80 cm, height of the pedestal 2.40 cm, diameter of fire pot 4.30 cm, diameter of base 3.90 cm, diameter of the hole for pipe 0.80 cm. (Pl.XXXI -6)

No.2. SKT-91, A1, Qd.3, A2 - 7.80 m, B2 - 3.20 m., depth 0.72 m, layer 5, Period III. Made of well levigated, well fired terracotta, dull red. Core is black; bottom is bulbous; neck constricted and the fire and tobacco container is in the form of a cup with outward flaring rim. The inner side is having deep soot marks whereas the outer surface of container is decorated with five horizontal lines in the lower portion and a band of four lines in the upper portion. In between the band of two lines there are small pinched circles.

The portion between the upper and lower bands of lines is decorated with close incised vertical lines. The hole in the centre of the fire pot goes all through the neck and bulbous base. The pot is attached to the pipe which leads to the basal pot containing water. In this case the smoke was not directly inhaled by the smoker but it passed through water which acted as filter for nicotine. Maximum height is 5.8 cm, outer diameter of fire pot is 3.6 cm. Diameter of the hole is 0.9 cm. (Pl.XXXI-4).

No.3 SKT-91, A1, Qd.4, A2 - 1.10 m., B2 - 9.20 m., depth 0.25 m, layer 2, Period VI. Made out of rough grained dark brown sandstone. A direct type hooka having flat base, cylindrical and solid pedestal and funnel shaped fire pot with featureless straight rim. The junction line of the two portions is decorated with thin beaded designs running horizontally all through the circle. At this point there is an oblique hole for attachment of the smoke pipe. Maximum height is 8.00 cm, height of fire pot is 4.5 cm, height of pedestal is 3.00 cm, thickness of beaded line is 0.5 cm, diameter of the smoke hole is 1.0 cm. (Pl.XXXI-2)

No.4. SKT-91, A1, Qd.2, A1 - 7.50 m, B1 - 5.70 m, depth 0.10 m, layer 2, Period VI. Made of well levigated, well fired clay just in the form of an ice-cream cup. The rounded flat base in the form of a ring is 0.5 cm thick, followed by a groove of equal thickness, topped by a bulbous 0.70 cm thick part and capped by the fire pot which is 3.00 cm high. The smoke hole is throughout broader towards bottom. The inner side of the fire pot is having a deep coat of soot indicating its frequent use. The outer surface of the fire pot is decorated like No.2, except for the difference that in the lower portion also between the bands of two lines there are circular, shallow pinched designs.

It is an indirect type of hooka similar to No.3, where the smoke was allowed first to pass through the water pot. Maximum height is 4.90 cm, diameter of fire pot is 4.20 cm. (Pl.XXXI-1)

No.5. SKT-91, A1, Qd.4, depth 7.0 m, layer 2, Period VI. Made of black terracotta, only the bulbous pedestal part with the hole for pipe is present. Convex bottom with a ring at the base; is maximum height is 1.90 cm, diameter of base is 3.1 cm, diameter of hole is 1.1 cm. (Pl.XXXI-5).

No.6. SKT-1/91. Surface. Made of dull red rough gained sandstone. The direct type having with solid pedestal rounded convex bottom. Sides of the fire pot are very thick and conical on inner side; featureless rim. The hole for pipe attachment is oblique and located at the junction of fire pot and base. Maximum height is 5.80 cm, height of base is 2.5 cm, height of fire pot is 3.3 cm, diameter of base is 3.8 cm, diameter of rim is 4.2 cm. (Pl.XXXI-3)

B. Metal Objects

Manipur has substantial deposits of copper ore. They are available near Ukhrul which has been exploited since centuries. Iron ore is also available both in the valley and upper reaches. There is substantial deposit of iron ore near the border town of Moreh. The plentiful finds of iron and copper/bronze objects from the burials right from the lowest levels to the top clearly indicate that both the ores were being exploited by the people of Manipur atleast from 2nd-3rd century B.C. onwards as per evidences obtained at Sekta. Burials at Sekta clearly prove that people were in possession of plenty of iron and copper-bronze objects. Their internment in large numbers in the burials shows that both the metals were easily available and people had the resources to acquire them. People of Sekta appear to be economically sound as almost all the burials had plenty of beads, rings, bangles, *ghungroos* and implements of iron. In some cases beautiful bronze pots and copper plates have also been interned. Copper was mostly used for preparation of masks to cover the skull that were given secondary burial inside the pots. Of the total metal objects recovered from all the levels copper-bronze account for 77.5% whereas iron objects account for 22.5%. The iron objects in the burials predominantly comprised of objects of attack and defence such as scythe, spear-heads and knife. Knives may be predominantly for use in household purposes as their size indicates. One harpoon head was also recovered. It is quite clear that copper-bronze ornaments like ear rings and finger rings were being used by both sexes whereas bangles (both wrist and arm) were mostly being used by women only. This fact could be brought out from the nature of internments of these objects along with other objects. The burial pots that contained iron objects of attack like spearheads, daggers and scythe did not contain copper-bronze bangles though rings both ear and or finger rings were found with them. This evidence has also helped us in deciding whether a particular burial belonged to a male or female though, of course due to heavy rains and nature of soil in the area, it was very difficult to differentiate and demarcate clearly individual burials as due to overlapping also grave furnitures of different burials, generally of the same level, got mixed up.

I. Iron objects (Pls. XXXIX to XLIII, Fig. 21)

Out of 204 metal objects recovered 47 were iron objects. All the iron objects are in a state of high corrosion and have developed numerous cracks. As the burial ground is just on the left bank of the River Iril and the entire deposit consists of fine silt and decomposed vegetational material, with the water table being very high (nearly 2.0 metres in the burial area) the soil remains always damp. The presence of high percentage of humidity and dampness has further aggravated the process of corrosion, decomposition and

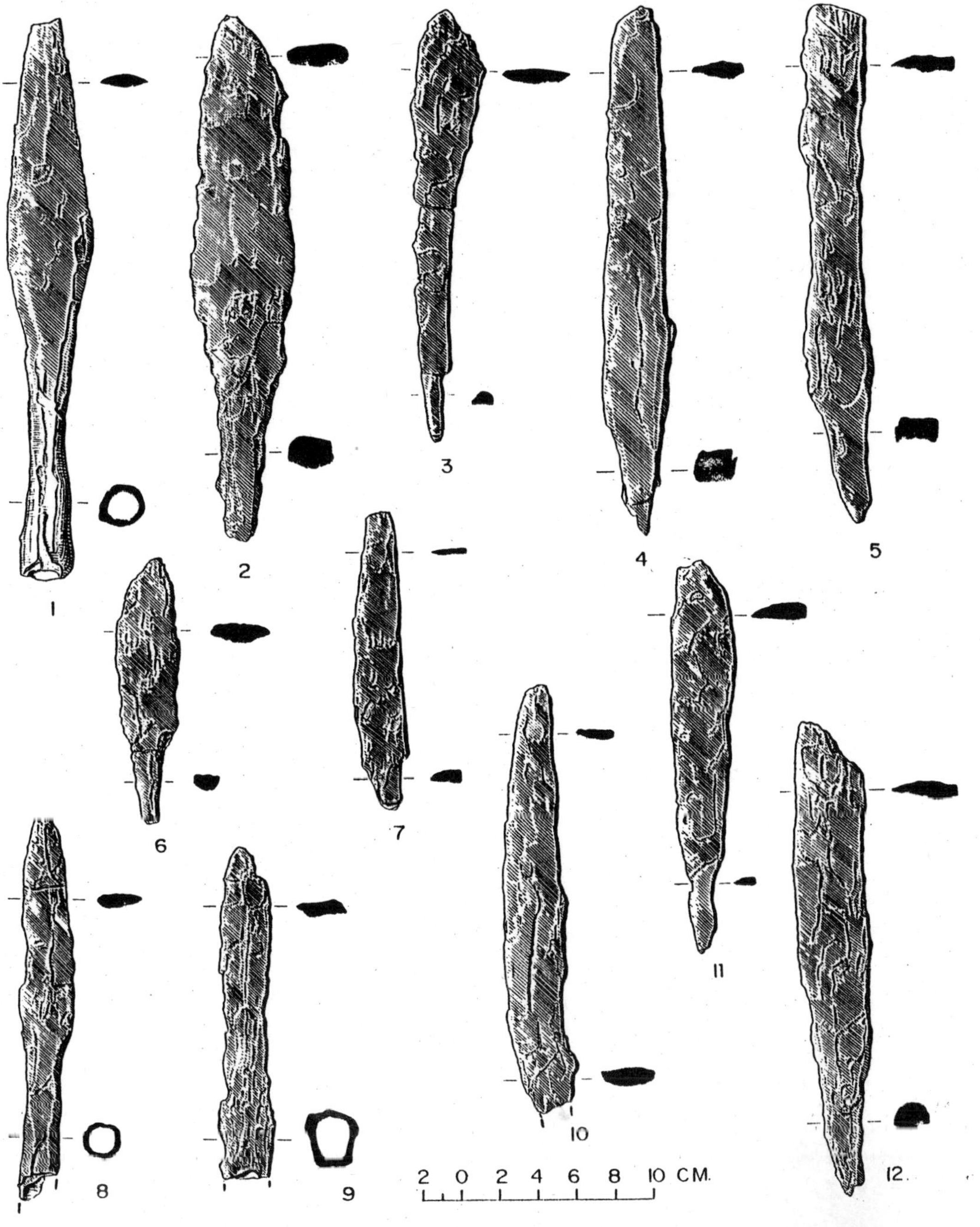

Fig. 21

disintegration, particularly of iron and copper objects. There is little effect of these on bronze objects.

Periodwise incidence

Objects	**Period**						
	I	II	III	IV	V	VI	VII
Ring -	-	-	-	1	1	1	-
Dagger and Knife	-	-	2	3	5	6	2
Scythe	-	-	-	1	-	-	2
Spear-head	-	-	1	4	3	5	1
Ball	-	-	-	-	-	1	-
Harpoon head	-	-	-	-	-	-	1
Unidentified	-	-	-	-	3	3	1
		Total	3	9	12	16	7

Note: As a very limited area was dug to the depth of Period I to III which yielded a few pot burials and as it was decided to preserve them in-situ for a site museum, contents from the pots of these periods were not removed.

From the above table it could be seen that spear-heads and knives, the two most common implements of use occur right from Period III to Period VII. Maximum number of objects were recovered from Period VI; this shows that most probably iron objects were much in use during this period.

Knowledge of iron technology gave the people of Manipur a distinct advantage over their enemies. There was no need to import the material as plenty of ore was available in the area. Moreover, it is quite clear that the people right from Period III knew the process of iron smelting. The simple method being used by tribals of Bastar in M.P. and other places was used. As the entire society was in need of this metal, particularly for purpose of defence, it is quite likely that the job was a speciality of a particular group of people as is the case in M.P. where in tribal areas the job of iron smithy is done by a particular sect of people called Agharias. Knife was generally the tool of household use as it is of smaller size. Total absence of any agricultural implement of iron from the burials does not necessarily indicate that iron tools were not in use for agricultural purposes as generally agricultural implements do not form part of grave furniture in other sites of different cultures, e.g.

Harappan burials at Lothal, Kalibangan, megalithic pot burials of Khuntitoli, etc. As no arrow heads have been recovered it is likely that the Manipuris of these periods did not prefer the use of bows and arrows for hunting instead they used spears which is a weapon of direct attack. Recovery of a harpoon head indicates that iron was in use for fishing and that too only in the last phases of the Sekta culture as one specimen was recovered from Period VII only.

a) Scythe or Sword

R.No.63 - From Period VII, long straight type with one edge sharp and the other blunt, triangular cross-section. Both the ends are broken. Maximum length is 33.2 cm, maximum width is 3.8 cm, at the hilt edge. Sides suddenly join at a sharp point. Heavily corroded. SKT-1, A1, Qd.1.

R.No.83 - From Period VII, long straight type with one edge sharp and the other blunt with conical handle. Triangular cross-section. Maximum length is 25.10 cm., maximum width is 3.90 cm., heavily corroded and flaking out. SKT-1, A1, Qd.2, (Pl.XXXIX-3, Fig.21-12).

R.No.216 - Form Period IV. A very long straight type with a gradually tapering conical handle. One edge is sharp and the other blunt; triangular cross-section. Pointed front is broken. Heavily corroded. Maximum length is 27.00 cm., maximum width is 3.6 cm. at the junction of the handle and working edge. SKT-1, A1, Qd.2 (Pl.XLII-1, Fig.21-5).

b) Spearheads

Spearheads are generally leaf shaped with flattish or slightly elliptical cross-section and hollow handles. Sides gradually taper towards the pointed end.

R.No.305 - Spearhead from Period V, heavily corroded and in several pieces A longish blade gradually tapering towards pointed end, lenticular in cross-section. Maximum length is 30.2 cm., maximum width is 3.2 cm., SKT-1, A1, Qd.3.

R.No.289 - Thrusting type spearhead from Period V with solid conical tang, rectangular cross-section, heavily made with a fore shaft. Dagger shaped long blade with a pointed tip. Maximum length is 23.3 cm., maximum width is 5.4 cm., SKT-1, A1, Qd.1 (Pl.XXXIX-4, Fig 21-2).

R.No.96 - A short conical and pointed spearhead with a hollow socketed base for insertion of wooden handle. Circular in cross-section, heavily corroded and broken into pieces. Maximum length is 15.4 cm., from Period VII, SKT-1, A1, Qd.4. (Pl.XL-3)

R.No.227 - A short leaf shaped spearhead from Period IV. Heavily corroded and in pieces. With a solid conical tang, cross-section bi-convex, both sharpened sides tapering into a fine point. SKT-1, A1, Qd.2. Maximum length is 12.90 cm., maximum width is 3.20 cm. (Pl.XLIII-3 and XXXVIII B)

R.No.341 - Spearhead from Period IV. A long flattish blade with lenticular section converging on top into a pointed tip. Hollow circular handle with circular cross-section. Maximum length is 22.30 cm., extant diameter of handle near base is 8.5 cm. SKT-1, A1, Qd.2. (Pl.XL-4, Fig.21-4)

R.No.119 - Spearhead from Period VI with long narrow blade sides running almost parallel and ending into a pointed tip, section of blade is biconvex whereas that of hollow socketed handle is circular. SKT-1, A1, Qd.1. Maximum length is 28.50 cm., external diameter of handle is o.5 cm. (Pl.XL-2)

R.No.325 - A short leaf shaped spearhead with a biconvex blade having sharp edges and point. A truncated solid conical handle having square cross-section. From Period III, SKT-1, A1, Qd.I. Maximum length is 14.00 cm., maximum width is 3.3 cm. (Fig.21-6)

R.No.318 - A long willow leaf shaped flattish spearhead with a round hollow stem at the lower end for insertion of a wooden handle. Cross-section of blade is double curved, whereas that of the handle is circular. From Period IV, Maximum length is 29.00 cm., maximum width is 4.4 cm., inner diameter of stem is 1.5 cm., outer diameter of stem is 2.8 cm., SKT-1, A1, Qd.1 (Pl.XL-5, Fig.21-1)

R.No.311 - A flattish long spearhead with a round hollow stem. The blade is having double convex cross-section whereas the handle is circular in cross-section. From Period V. Maximum length is 19.9 cm., maximum width of blade is 2.9 cm., outer diameter of stem is 2.0 cm., SKT-1, A1, Qd.3 (Pl.XLII-3, Fig 21-8)

(Similar to Nagda, Period III - 600-200 B.C.)

No.111 - A short flat bladed spearhead with a pointed tip and a round hollow stem. Cross-section of blade is rectangular whereas that of the stem is circular. Heavily corroded. From Period VI. Maximum length is 17.00 cm., maximum width of blade is 2.6 cm, diameter (outer) of stem is 2.7 cm., SKT-1, A1, Qd.1. (Pl.XLII-2, Fig 21-9).

R.No.331 - Spearhead with solid tang for hafting on a handle, lenticular cross-section, two sides gradually tapering to a pointed end. From Period VI. Maximum length is 20.5 cm., maximum width is 2.9 cm., SKT-1, A1, Qd.2.

R.No.342 - A heavily corroded short spearhead from Period IV, tip and end of solid tang is broken. It is leaf shaped having lenticular cross-section, both the margins are sharp and taper to a point. Maximum length is 8.5 cm., maximum width is 3.4 cm. SKT-1, A1, Qd.3. (Pl.XLI-5).

c) Daggers and Knives

Knives with blades having a short tang and circular section came into use during the Megalithic period as is revealed from the finds at Takalghat, Khapa, Sanur and Brahmagiri.

In the Early historical period two types were fairly common, viz. concave backed and with straight back and tapering edge. The former type has been found at sites like Nasik, Kausambi, Besnagar, Maheshwar, Nevasa, Jorwe, Nagara and Sisupalgarh. The earliest among these are from Nasik, assignable to the period between 300 B.C. and A.D.400. Knives from Ahar are with tapering end, one edge sharp and the other blunt. Iron knives were extensively used in the Indo-Roman period (1st century B.C. to 2nd-3rd century A.D.).

R.No.152 - Dagger from Period VI, incomplete, heavily corroded, of longish blade, apparently sharp parallel sides abruptly tapering to form a sharp point, lenticular in cross-section. Maximum length is 21.6 cm., maximum width, is 3.3 cm. SKT-1, A1, Qd.4.

No.139 - Dagger from Period V, incomplete, heavily corroded, of longish blade with sharp parallel sides and having hollow socket to be inserted in a wooden handle, lenticular cross-section in the blade region, whereas circular in the handle region. Maximum length is 17.8 cm., maximum width is 2.8 cm., SKT-1, A1, Qd.2.

R.No.176 - Knife blade fragment from Period V, working edge crescent shaped whereas opposite edge is almost squarish in section, maximum length is 6.0 cm., maximum width is 2.6 cm., SKT-1, A1, Qd.2.

R.No.212 - Knife from Period V, working edge is crescent shaped while the other is straight, with solid tapering tang at one edge. Maximum length is 6.8 cm., maximum width is 1.8 cm. SKT-1, A1, Qd.2 (Pl.XLI-6).

Similar to the one found at Tripuri (Fig.21-3), Stratum IV (100 B.C. to A.D. 200)

R.No.84 - Knife from Period VII. Fragment, tanged with a curved blade, tang at one edge. Maximum length is 8.3 cm., maximum width is 2.9 cm., SKT-1, A1, Qd.2.

R.No.254 - Knife, tang solid with a curved blade, working edge is crescent shaped, cross-section is triangular. Maximum length is 9.8 cm., maximum width 2.6 cm. From Period IV, SKT-1, A1, Qd.2.

R.No.175 - Knife from Period V. tanged with curved blade, tang solid, tapering down from the blunt edge; working edge crescent shaped. Maximum length is 12.90 cm., maximum width is 2.90 cm. SKT-1, A1, Qd.2. (Pl.XLI-3).

Similar to Tripuri Fig.38-3, stratum IV (100 B.C. to A.D. 200).

R.No.280 - Knife in three pieces, heavily corroded, from Period VI. Triangular cross-section with crescent shaped working edge, handle pointed and solid. Maximum length is 17.1 cm., maximum width is 2.2 cm., SKT-1, A1, Qd.3.

R.No.332 - Knife has a long blade; working edge is crescent shaped; triangular cross-section. From Period VI, is heavily corroded and in pieces, maximum length is 16.7 cm., maximum width is 2.6 cm., SKT-1, A1, Qd.2.

R.No.282 - Hollow handle of javelin or spearhead from Period VI. Heavily corroded, end is circular in section, having an inner diameter of 1.7 cm., maximum length is 7.6 cm., circular in cross-section. SKT-1, A1, Qd.4.

R.No.162 - Knife from Period VI, solid tang, corner blade with slightly upturned tip, triangular cross-section. Maximum length is 6.2 cm., maximum width is 2.5 cm., SKT-1, A1, Qd.4.

R.No.266 - Knife from Period IV. Tanged with a curved blade, triangular cross-section, heavily corroded. Maximum length is 7.4 cm., maximum width is 2.2 cm. SKT-1, A1, Qd.2.

R.No.170 - Knife from Period V, tanged with a curved convex back, cross-section is triangular, is heavily corroded, tip is broken. Maximum length is 7.4 cm, maximum width is 2.3 cm. SKT-1, A1, Qd.2.

R.No.231 - Hollow handle of spearhead or Javelin from Period VI. Circular in cross-section but tapering towards a closed rounded bottom. Maximum length is 9.1 cm., SKT-1, A1, Qd.4.

R.No.281 - Knife from Period VI. Long knife with a convex sharp cutting edge and straight thick opposite edge; working edge ending in a rounded tip. It appears as if it was having a solid conical handle; triangular cross-section; heavily corroded. Maximum length is 21.4 cm., maximum width is 3.1 cm. SKT-1, A1, Qd.3. (Fig. 21-10, Pl.XLI-4).

R.No.48 - Knife from Period VII. A maximum sized straight knife with both the edges parallel. Sharp working edge ending in a sharp point. Triangular in cross-section. Dimensions 14.0 x 2.30 x 0.60 cm. SKT-1, A1, Qd.4. (PL.XLI-2). It is similar to the one found from Stratum V (A.D. 200-400) at Tripuri.[1]

R.No.265 - Knife from Period IV. Heavily corroded with handle missing. Longish blade with sharp side ending into a sharp point; cross-section is triangular. Dimensions - 19.60 x 3.30 x 1.10 cm. SKT-1, A1, Qd.2.(Pl.XLIII-4)

R.No.153 - Knife from Period VI. A long almost parallel sided knife suddenly

1. Dikshit, M.G. - Tripuri, 1952, Fig. 38-2.

ending into a pointed tip. Triangular cross-section, solid conical handle. Due to its extraordinary length and heavy weight it appears to be a dagger with only one edge sharp and the other blunt and squarish. Maximum length is 27.00 cm., maximum width near the handle junction is 3.6 cm. SKT-1, A1, Qd.4. (Fig.21-4, PL.XXXIX-2).

R.No.355 - Knife from surface collection, long knife with a convex sharp cutting edge and straight thick opposite edge, tip is broken; conical short handle, triangular in cross-section; heavily corroded. Maximum length is 15.30 cm., maximum width is 2.5 cm.

R.No.356 - Knife from surface collection. In the lower half of the blade both sides run parallel but later on they broaden to form a shot of elongated oval. Upper half having a rounded sharp end. Both sides appear to be sharp thus actually acting as a dagger. Cross-section lenticular, maximum length is 22. 7 cm., maximum width at the point of junction of back and handle is 1.7 cm. The solid, conical handle with round section emerges in a straight line from one of the endges. SKT-1. (Fig.21-3, Pl.XLII-4).

R.No.345 - Knife, from Period III, heavily corroded, only fragment is left; working edge is crescent shaped whereas the other edge is blunt and squarish, nearly lenticular cross-section. Maximum length is 7.4 cm., maximum width is 2.8 cm. SKT-1, A1, Qd.3.

R.No.343 - Blade of a longish knife from Period III, heavily corroded and only half fragment is available; almost squarish cross-section; working edge slightly crescent shaped. Maximum length is 8.6 cm., maximum width is 2.7 cm. SKT-1, A1, Qd.3.

d) Miscellaneous

R.No.173 - Bangle or ring. Only half present, heavily corroded. From Period V. Circular cross-section. Maximum diameter is 6.00 cm. Maximum thickness is 1.3 cm. SKT-1, A1, Qd.2. (Pl.XLI-8).

R.No.253 - Ring from Period IV, fragment heavily corroded, circular cross-section. Maximum thickness is 1.3 cm., SKT-1, A1, Qd.2..

R.No.182 - Ring. Flat with rectangular cross-section. Height 1.2 cm., thickness 0.3, inner diameter 2.6 cm. From Period VI. SKT-1, A1, Qd.IV.

R.No.25 - Harpoon from Period VII. Single barbed with hollow socket for insertion in a long handle, tip missing, barbed edge very sharp. Maximum length is 4.2 cm., inner diameter of socket is 0.4 cm. On reconstruction maximum length is 5.6 cm., SKT-1, A1, Qd.1 (Pl.XLI-7).

II Copper and Bronze (Pls. XLIV to XLVIII)

Copper and bronze objects interned with the burials, mostly comprise of bangles, rings (both finger and ear), plates, masks, *gunghroo* and some utensils like bowl, vase and relic casket. The assemblage predominates in bangles and rings and that too a majority are shaped out of brass. Copper objects are very few. Masks and plates have been shaped out of thin sheets of copper as brass is not suitable for preparation of thin sheets and could also not be given the desired shape and contours which is required for preparation of face masks. As bronze is a more durable material corrosionwise, most of the objects have been found in good condition though some have broken into pieces as the metal has no elasticity and tensile strength. Copper objects recovered are in very fragile condition with the bleaching out of copper sulphate due to reaction with the soil. Almost all the objects in burials were found interned inside earthern pots along with fragments of human bones or in some cases masked human skull and associated with iron objects and plenty of beads. The objects were generally kept inside the main big jar. Only in few cases they were kept inside smaller earthern vessels.

A. Bangles

Bangles of shell, terracotta, copper and bronze, both plain and decorated, are of widespread occurrence at the Early and Late historical sites throughout the country. They could be divided into the following types:

1) Closed, 2) Open, 3) Single Coil,
4) Multi coiled, 5) Simple, 6) Decorated,
7) Solid, 8) Hollow.

Cross–Section - 1) Circular, 2) Rectangular 3) Plano-convex.

BANGLES & BRACELETS

Period	**II**	**III**	**IV**	**V**	**VI**	**VII**
Copper	-	-	-	-	-	2
Bracelet						
Bangle	-	-	-	3	5	1
Bronze						
Bracelets	-	-	-	-	2	-
Bangles	-	-	6	6	9	6

a) Copper

In all seven copper bangles were recovered; one from Period VII, three from Period VI and three from Period V. From other Periods copper bangles were not found. Out of the seven specimens, five are of open type and two are of closed type. Both the closed ones are hollow also. All, except one which has a rectangular cross-section, others are having circular cross-section. Both hollow types were recovered from the same burial pot indicating that they belonged to a single individual. These hollow ones are actually not bangles, but are bracelets generally worn by ladies one in each wrist along with bangles.

R.No.271 - Copper, complete bracelet from Period VI. Plano-convex in section with inner circle plain; closed and hollow type; shaped out of copper plate by curving the two edges of the plate inside. Might have been used as an armlet as well. Inner diameter is 6.6 cm., thickness is 0.90 cm. Decorated with three circular incised grooves at the false closing ends, both sides of which have been further decorated with tendril designs. SKT-1, A1, Qd.3. (Pl.XLIV-1).

R.No.273 - Same as No.271 but in two pieces. From Period VI. Both were recovered from the same burial pot. Inner diameter 6.6 cm., thickness is 0.90 cm. SKT-1,A1, Qd.3.

R.No.106 - Copper bangle, complete but twisted; open ends and solid type, made of wire, circular in cross-section, heavily encrusted with copper sulphate. From Period VI. Inner diameter is 4.1 cm., thickness is 0.40 cm., SKT-1, A1, Qd.4 (Pl.XLIV-6).

R.No.167 - Copper, open ends type. Circular in cross-section, solid, heavily corroded, inner diameter is 3.1 cm., thickness is 0.4 cm. Period V. SKT-1, A1, Qd.4. (Pl.XLIV-7).

R.No.127 - Copper, open ends, solid type. Circular in cross-section, inner diameter is 2.9 cm., thickness is 0.4 cm., Period VII. SKT-1, A1, Qd.2. (Pl.XLIV-5).

R.No.168 - Copper bangle, open ends, coiled, solid type with circular crross section; heavily corroded, straight cut ends. Inner diameter is 3.2 cm., thickness is 0.5 cm., Period V. SKT-1, A1, Qd.2. (Pl.XLIV-8).

R.No.291 - Copper bangles, open ends, solid type made out of plate; rectangular cross-section; one end riding over the other; heavily corroded. Inner diameter is 4.3 cm., thickness is 0.15 cm. Period V. SKT-1, A1, Qd.1, (Pl.XLIV-2).

b) Bronze

In all there are thirty brass bangles including two bracelets or wristlets. They are all solid types with generally circular or in a few cases plano convex cross-section. Except four which are of open, coiled type, all the others are of closed type. The two wristlets are of open type. Almost all the closed types are decorated with circular grooves and knot designs in imitation of those of their predecessors of non-metallic age that were made out of thin bamboo slices or twigs when it was necessary to tie both the ends with thread or very thin strings of bamboo or twig as the case may be. This is indicative of continued tradition as the phenomenon is also seen in caves excavated at Karla-Bhaja and various south Indian temples where wooden architecture has been copied in stone also, honestly imitating the details of wooden designs and decorations. In certain tribal areas and remote villages of India, girls from poor families could even now be seen wearing bangles, ear rings, bracelets, etc. made by themselves out of bamboo slices, twigs and leguminous fruits of *Accacia arabica* or Babool.

Out of twentyeight pieces of bangles, twentyfive are of closed, solid type with decorations of the above mentioned design and with circular cross-section. Majority of them, i.e. eighteen are in pieces whereas seven are complete. Of this type four are from Period VII, nine from Period VI, five from Period V, six from Period IV and one from Period III. There are three open, coiled type, three with circular corss section and one with plano-convex cross-section. Out of these two belong to Period VII, and one from Period IV. The specimens from Period III, i.e. Reg. No.338 are actually two bangles but due to heavy corrosion and oozing out of ferric oxide from adjacent iron object of the same burial, they have stuck together and difficult to seperate. In a number of cases from each burial two bangles were recovered, e.g. 294 and 295, 223 and 224, 186 and 187, etc. There are two solid open type of armlets from Period VI coming from the same burial pot. They are having circular cross-section.

R.Nos.145 & 146 - Bronze, armlets or wristlets of solid open type. Circular in cross-section. Both from Period VI. 145 - inner diameter is 6.7 cm., thickness is 0.50 cm. SKT-1, A1, Qd.4. (Pl.XLIV-9).

R.No.242 - Bronze, open, solid type, one end riding over the other, plano-convex cross-section. Inner diameter is 3.5 cm., thickness is 0.20 cm. Period V. SKT-1, A1, Qd.1.

R.No.58 - Bronze, open, coiled, solid, circular cross-section, coils overlap upto half of the circle. Inner diameter is 4.2 cm., thickness is 0.40 cm. Period VII, SKT-1,A1, Qd.4.

R.No.57 - Bronze, open, coiled, solid, circular cross-section, the two coils making almost a double coil. Inner diameter is 3.8 cm., thickness is 0.30 cm.

Period VII. SKT-1, A1, Qd.4.

R.No.338 - Bronze, closed, solid type with plano-convex cross-section. In fact two bangles are sticking to each other. Outer diameter is 4.4 cm., thickness is 0.20 cm. Period III. SKT-1, A1, Qd.1.

R.No.225 - Bronze, closed, solid type, circular in cross-section. At false closing ends both sides are decorated with circular thread like designs ending into horizontal concentric circles with the outer circles of both touching each other. Inner diameter is 4.9 cm., thickness is 0.30 cm. Period IV. SKT-1, A1, Qd.2. (Pl.XLIV-4)

R.No.284 - Bronze, closed, solid, circular cross-section. Ends are joining in the form of tied up decoration with thin wired ending in a knot. Inner diameter is 3.9 cm., thickness is 0.20-0.30 cm. Period V. (Pl.XLIV-10)

R.No.187 - Bronze, closed solid type cirrcular cross-section, Ends are closed and decorated on both sides with coils ending in the form of two oval loops each. Inner diameter is 5.8 cm., thickness is 0.30 - 0.50 cm. Period VI. SKT-1, A1, Qd.2 (Pl.XLIV-3)

R.No.66 - Bronze, thin, closed, solid type, with circular cross-section. Both ends are closed and decorated with circular thread designs ending in a knot. Inner diameter is 4.6 cm., thickness is 0.20 cm. SKT-1, A1, Qd.4 (Pl.XLIV-II)

B. Rings

A large number of rings of copper and bronze, both decorated and plain have been recovered from the burial pots. They comprise of finger rrings and ear/nose rings. Like bangles, they are either of cirrcular cross-section or of plano-convex cross-section or of rectangular cross-section. Both closed and open types either with single circle or of a number of coiled circles are available. In copper both finger as well as ear/nose rings are available whereas in bronze only finger rings are found, as bronze is not a suitable metal for use in delicate parts like nose and ear due to its non elastic nature and heavy weight. For piercing through the soft skin of nose or ear-lobe copper is suitable as it could be made into a sharp point and pathologically it does not cause any infection to the skin. It is for this reason that according to Hindu traditions ears of male child and nose and ears of female child used to be pierced by the family goldsmith with a thin copper wire. The copper wire, in the form of a ring, was allowed to remain in position in the pierced hole of nose or ear till the wound healed. Only after complete healing ornaments were allowed to be worn. The size of the bronze rings indicate that they were used in the fingers of both hands and feet. Even today throughout the country in rural areas and also in some urban areas women wear rings, in their toes. In Chattisgarh region of Madhya Pradesh these toe rings are called *Chutki*. *Chutki* means the sound emitted by rubbing thumb and middle finger. While walking these toe rings in the feet emit a mild sound so they are called *Chutki.*

Rings - Periodwise Incidence

	Finger Rings						Ear/Nose rings			
Period	**II**	**III**	**IV**	**V**	**VI**	**VII**	**IV**	**V**	**VI**	**VII**
Copper										
Single coil	-	-	3	-	1	1	5	3	2	3
Multi coil	-	-	1	-	6	1				
Bronze										
Single coil	1	1	11	13	17	7				
Multicoil	-	-	1	1	2	2				

a) Copper

i) Finger Rings - In all there are thirteen copper finger rings. Out of these eight are of multi-coil type whereas four are single coil type. All are open. Open type has the advantage of adjustment, i.e. the diameter could be increased or decreased as per requirement. Copper finger rings start occurring right from Period IV. Maximum number of all types of rings have been recovered from Period VI.

Single Coil type

R.No.263 - Copper ring from Period IV.Single coil, open, rectangular cross-section, outer vertical face decorated with double oblique grooved lines forming 'V' designs. Internal diameter is 2.0 cm., thickness is 0.10 cm. SKT-1, A1, Qd.2. (Pl.XLV-5)

R.No.250 - Same as No.263,but highly corroded. Internal diameter is 2.20 cm., thickness, is 0.10 cm. Period IV. SKT-1, A1, Qd.2 (Pl.XLV-6).

Along with it another ring No.251, exactly similar to the one described was recovered from the same burial pot.

R.No.126 - Copper ring, single coil, open, plano-convex cross-section, heavily corroded from Period VII. Outer diameter is 2.1 cm., thickness is 0.20 cm. SKT-1, A1, Qd.2. (Pl.XLV-7).

Multicoil type

R.No.132 - Copper ring, open, coils over riding nearly upto half distance, rectangular cross-section, heavily corroded, from Period VI. Outer diameter is 1.6 cm., thickness is 0.15 cm., height is 0.40 cm. SKT-1, A1, Qd.2 (Pl.XLV-2).

XLI. Iron objects.

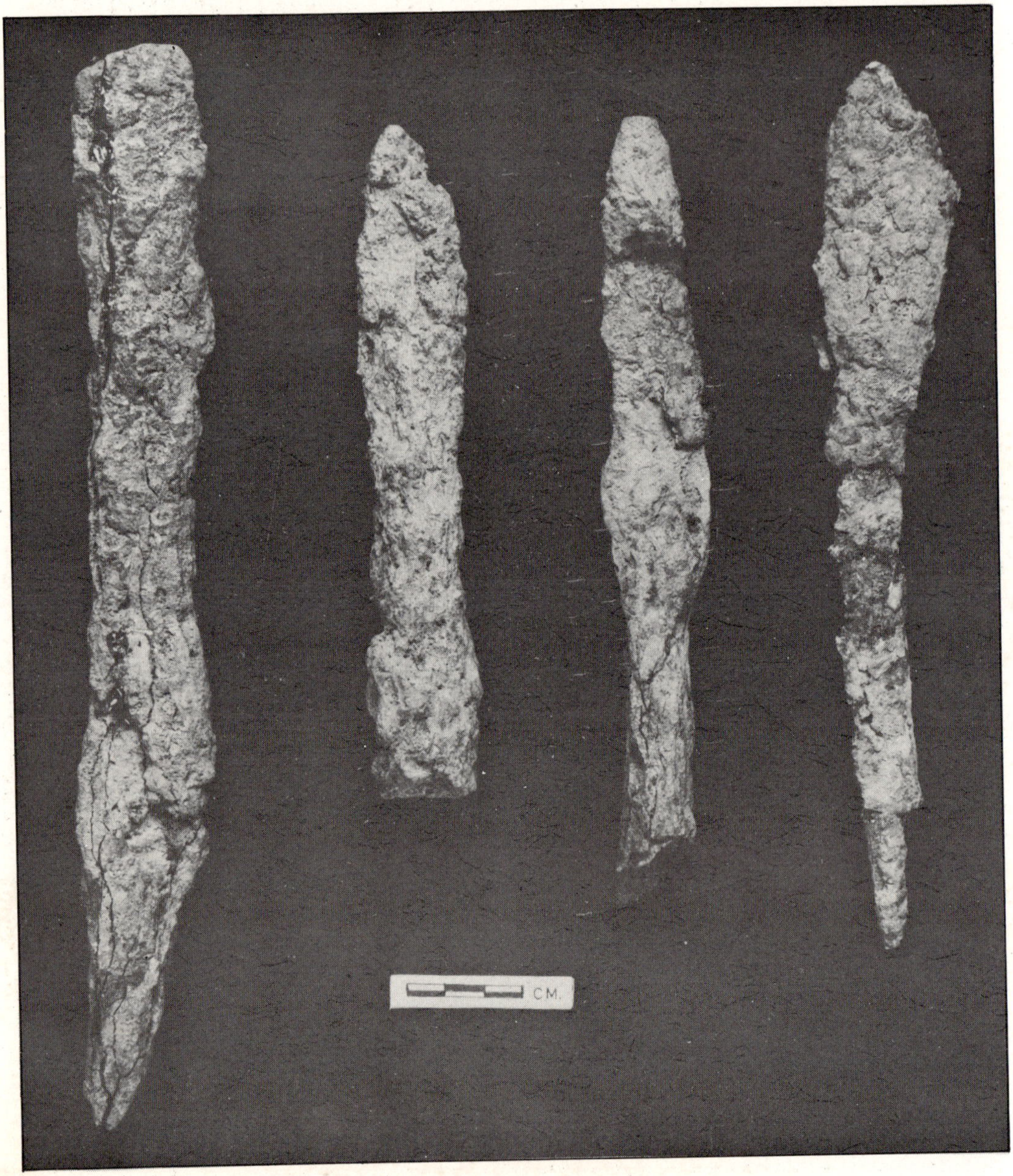

XLII. Iron objects.

XLIII. Iron objects.

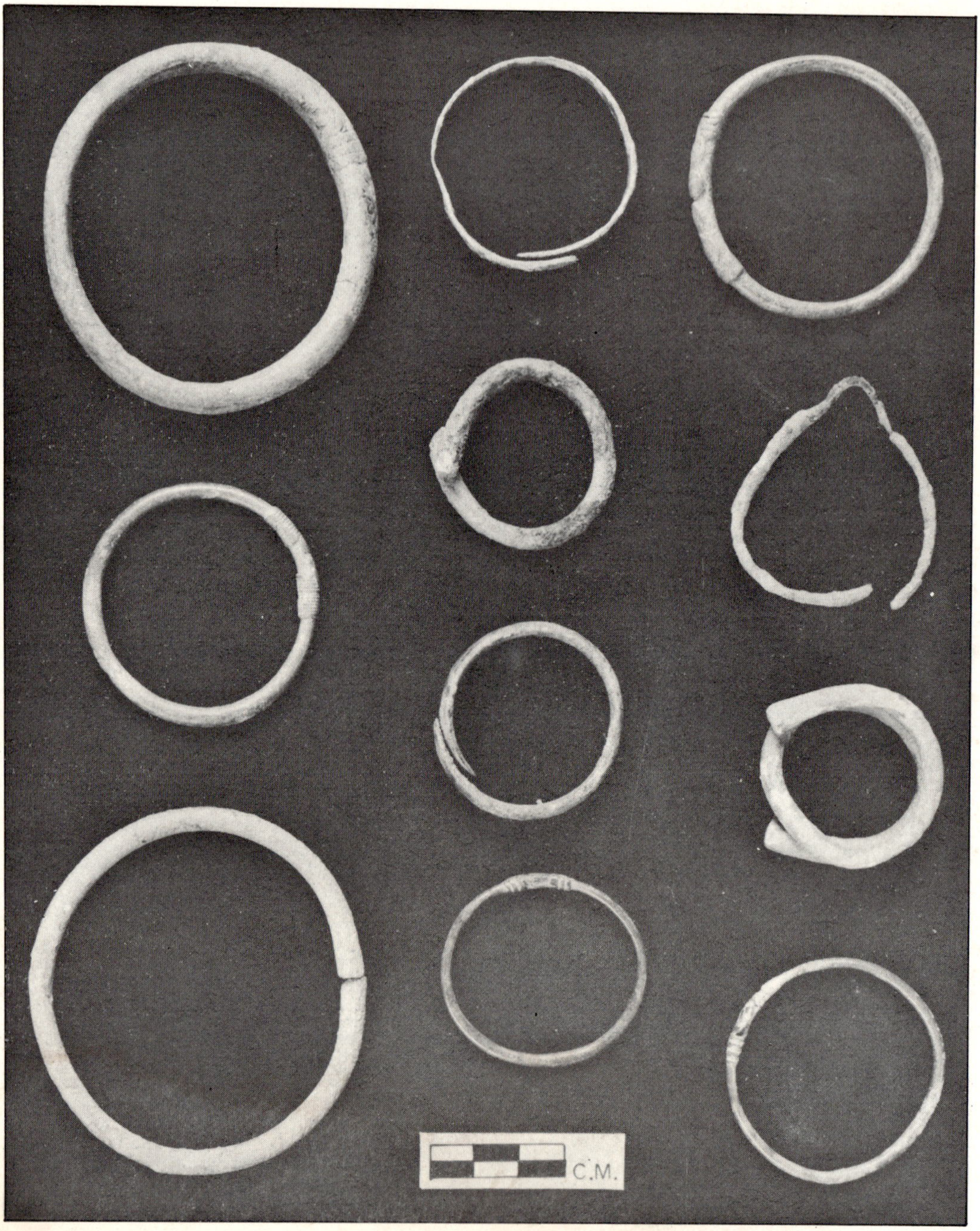

XLIV. Copper and bronze bangles.

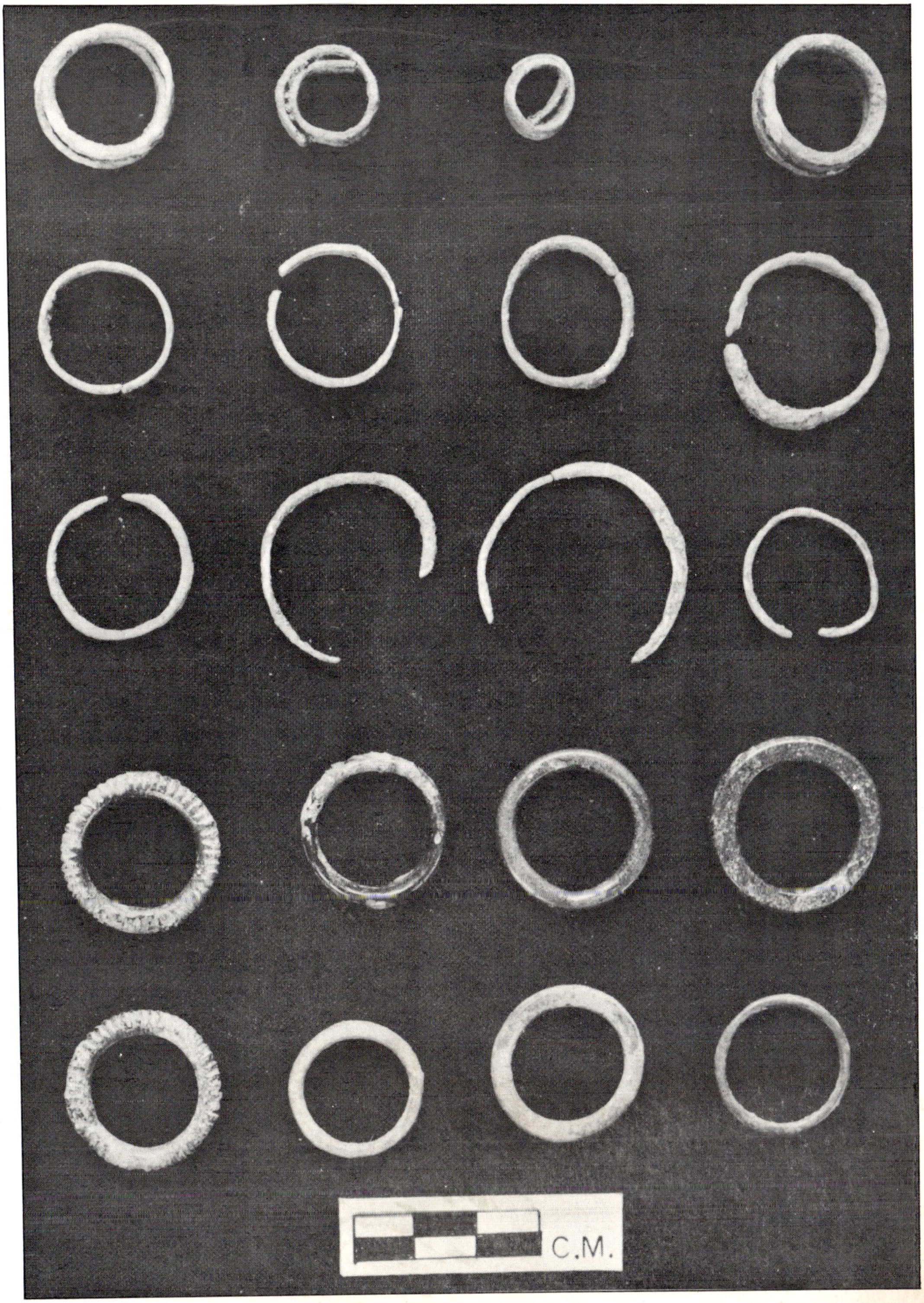

XLV. Copper and bronze rings.

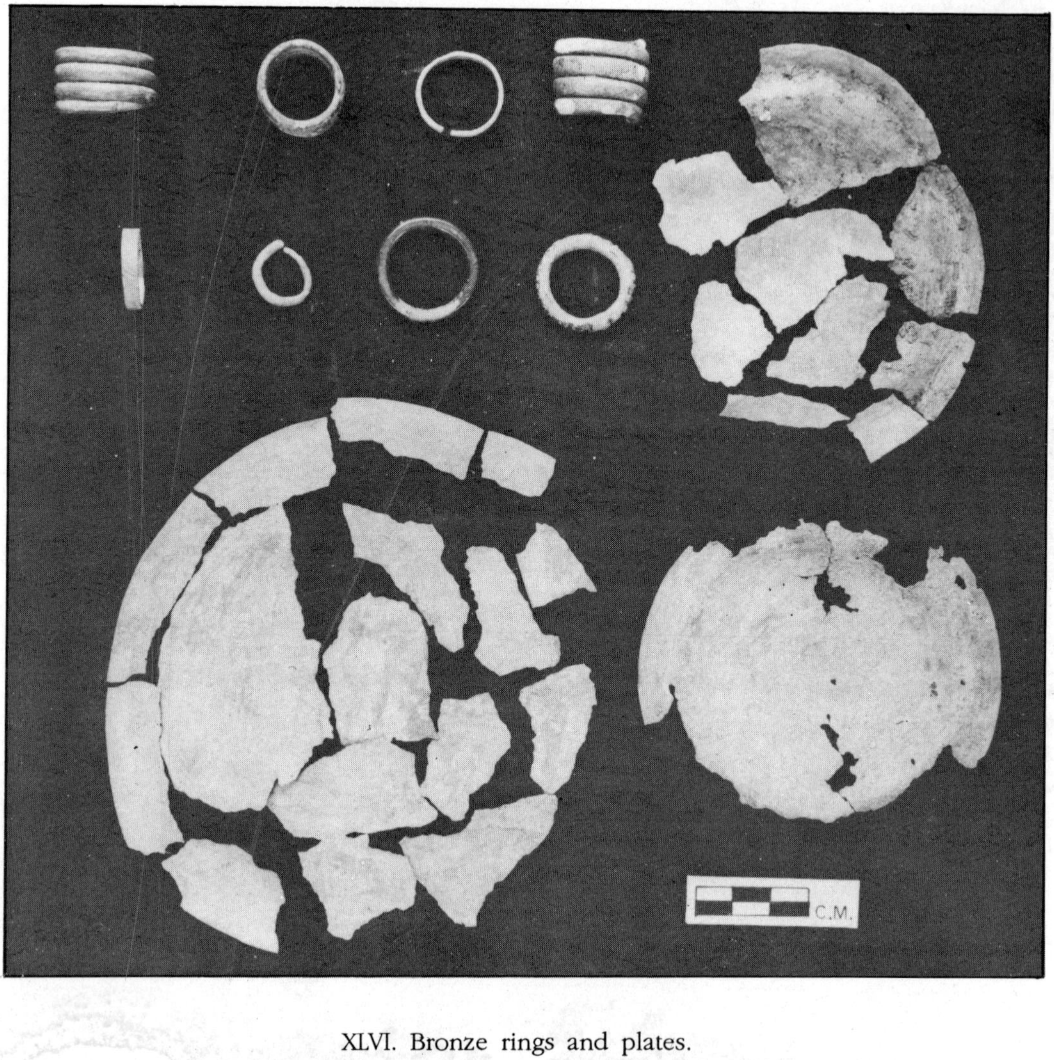

XLVI. Bronze rings and plates.

XLVII. Bronze A. Bowl, B. Flower vase.

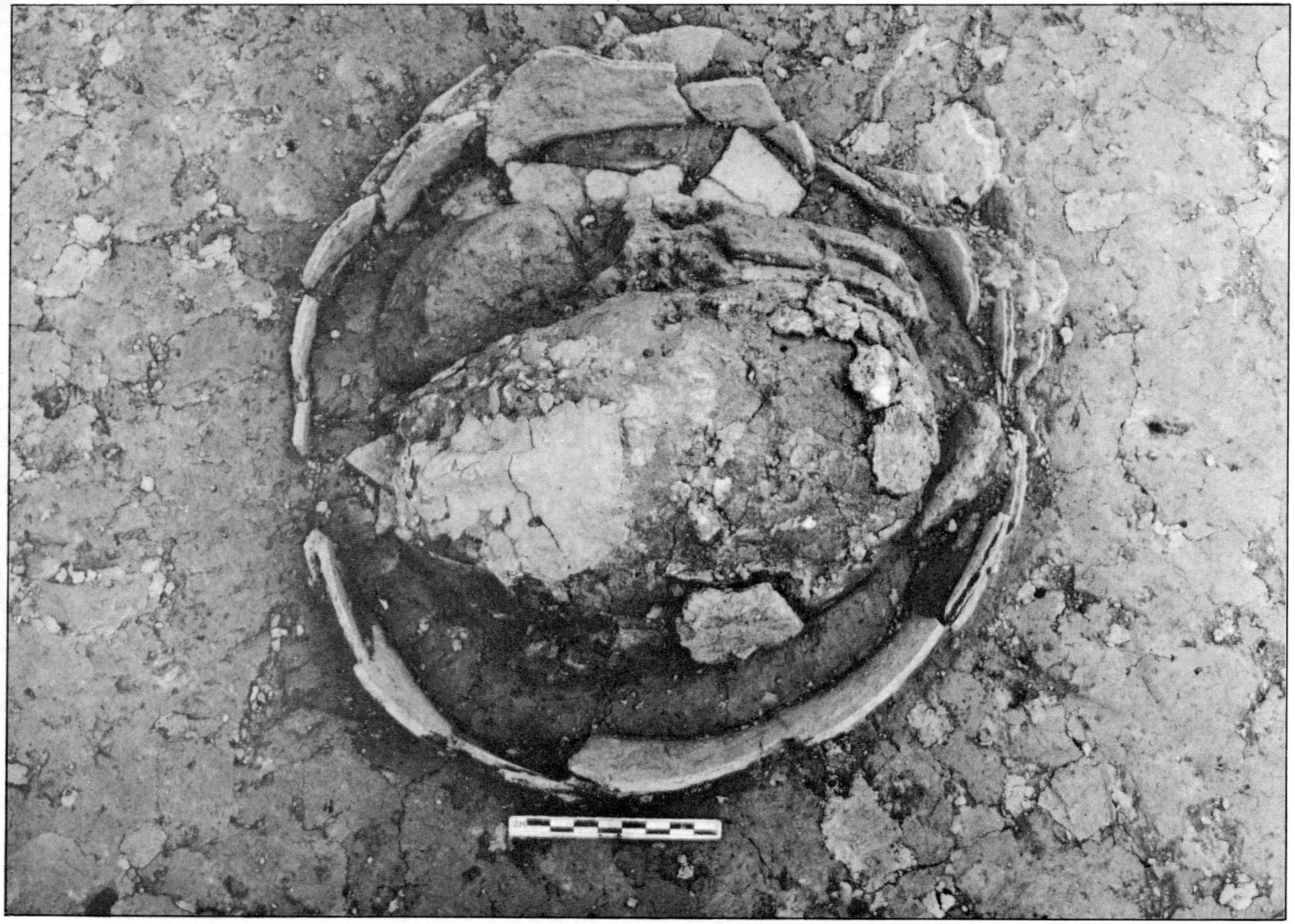

XLVIII. Copper masked human skull, another view.

R.No.118 - Copper ring, double coiled, rectangular cross-section, ends straight cut from Period VI. Outer diameter is 2.1 cm. Thickness of each coil is 0.20 cm., height of each coil is 0.35 cm. SKT-1, A1, Qd.1. (Pl.XLV4).

R.No.184 - Copper ring, double coiled, open, both ends are pointed, rectangular cross-section, from Period VI. Outer diameter is 2.1 cm., thickness is 0.20 cm., height of each coil is 0.15 cm. SKT-1,A1, Qd.4. (Pl.XLV-1).

R.No.61 - Copper ring, double coil, open, very small may be for a child's finger. Plano-convex cross-section From Period VII. Outer diameter is 1.7 cm., thickness is 0.15 cm., height is 0.35 cm. SKT-1, A1, Qd.4 (Pl.XLV-3).

ii) Ear/Nose rings

Out of thirteen ear/nose rings found only four are nose rings and rest are ear rings. Nose rings are generally very thin and small except in a few cases where large nose rings are used particularly on festive occassions. Three of the nose rings are from Period IV and one from Period V. From later periods, i.e. VI & VII nose rings were not recovered probably indicating that the custom of wearing nose rings had ceased. All the ear rings are thicker in the middle and slowly thin down towards the open ends.

R.No. 346 - Copper nose ring, very thin, circular in section, ends are pointed. Outer diameter is 2.1 cm., thickness is 0.10 cm. from Period IV.SKT-1, A1, Qd.3, (Pl.XLV-12).

R.No. 171 - Copper nose ring, circular cross-section, made of wire, outer diameter is 1.9 cm., thickness is 0.10 cm., from Period V. SKT-1, A1, Qd.2.

R.No.128 - Copper ear ring of *Bala* type. Plano-convex cross-section, outer diameter is 2.9 cm., thickness is 0.15 cm., from Period VII. SKT-1, A1, Qd.2 (Pl.XLV 10).

R.No.326 - Copper ear ring made of wire, circular cross-section, outer diameter is 2.6 cm., thickness is 0.10 cm. From Perod V. SKT-1, A1, Qd.2.

R.No.220 - Copper ear-ring, made of wire, circular cross-section, outer diameter is 2.30 cm., thickness is 0.10 cm. From Period IV. SKT-1, Qd.2. (Pl.XLV.9)

R.No.134 - Copper ear ring. Circular in cross-section, in pieces, thicker in the middle but very thin at both the open ends. Outer diameter is 3.5 cm., thickness is 0.20 cm. From Period VI.SKT-1, A1, Qd.2. (Pl.XLV-11)

(b) Bronze

(i) Finger Rings

In bronze a total of 56 finger rings were recovered. They are of the following types:

a) Simple, (b) Decorated, (c) Single coil, (d) double coil. They are either of circular or of plano-convex cross-section or of rectangular cross-section. Both thin and thick varieties are avialable. They start occurring right from Period II but are found in larger numbers from Period IV onwards, maximum being from Period VI.

R.No.172 - Bronze finger ring, small, open, circular cross-section. One end thinner than the other. Outer diameter is 1.7 cm., thickness is 0.20 cm., From Period V, SKT-1, A1, Qd.2. (Pl.XLVI-6)

R.No.262 - Bronze finger ring open, rectangular cross-section. Outer diameter is 1.90 cm., thickness is 0.15 cm., height is 0.40 cm. The outer surface is decorated with oblique double incised lines, throughout. From Period IV. SKT-1, A1, Qd.2. (Pl.XLVI-5)

Decorated, with circular cross-section

R.No.255 - Bronze finger ring, closed, circular section, decorated with semi-circular grooves (ridges and furrows) throughout the outer thickness. Outer diameter is 2.50 cm., thickness is 0.40 cm., From Period IV. SKT-1, A1, Qd.2. (Pl.XLV-13)

R.NO.314 - Bronze finger ring, closed and decorated. Similar to No.255. Outer diameter is 2.6 cm, thickness is 0.40 cm. From Period V, SKT-1, A-1, Qd-4 (Pl.XLVI-8)

R.No.256 - Bronze finger ring, closed and decorated on outer surface with semi-circular grooves. Circular in cross-section. Outer is diameter 2.50 cm., thickness is 0.40 cm. From Period IV. SKT-1, A1, Qd.2. (Pl.XL-17)

Plain with squarish cross-section but convex top.

R.No.1 - Bronze finger ring, plain, closed, cross-section square with top convex. From Period VII. Outer is diameter 2.70 cm., thickness is 0.40 cm. SKT-1, A1, Qd.2. (Pl.XLV-15)

R.No.352 - Bronze finger ring as No.1, plain, closed. Cross-section square with top convex. From Period II. Greenish black in colour, very smooth and shining, polished. Outer diameter is 2.8 cm., thickness is 0.40 cm. SKT-1, A1, Qd.2. (Pl.XLVI-7)

R.No.323 - Bronze finger ring, plain, closed having double convex cross-section, greenish-black, well polished, From Period IV. Outer diameter is 2.50 cm., thickness is 0.40 cm. SKT-1, A1, Qd.1. (Pl.XLV-14)

R.No. 201 - Bronze finger ring, plain, closed with squarish section, greenish in colour. Outer diameter is 2.5 cm., thickness is 0.40 cm. From Period V. SKT-1, A1, Qd.2, (Pl.XLV-19)

R.No.270 - Bronze finger ring, plain, closed, cross-section squarish, outer diameter is 2.30 cm., thickness is 0.03 cm, From Period VI, SKT-1, A1, Qd.3. (Pl.XLV-18).

R.No.125 - Bronze finger ring, plain, closed, thick, greenish black, well polished, square cross-section. From Period VII. Outer diameter is 2.8 cm., thickness is 0.50 cm. SKT-1, A1, Qd.2. (Pl.XLV-16)

R.No.130 - Bronze finger ring, plain, closed, thin greyish in colour circular cross-section. From Period VI. Outer diameter is 2.30 cm., thickness is 0.25 cm. SKT-1, A1, Qd.2 (Pl.XLV-20)

R.NO.350 - Bronze finger ring, plain, closed, thick, corroded, round in cross-section, from Period III. Outer diameter is 2.70 cm. SKT-1, A1, Qd.3.

Coiled type

R.No.197 - Bronze finger ring, coiled having four coils, simple, greenish in colour, very heavy, both the free ends of the coil tapering into points. It might have been used as toe ring for the finger of the feet. From Peroid V. Outer diameter is 2.5 cm., thickness is 0.040 cm., height 1.50 cm. SKT-1, Qd.1 (Pl.XLVI-1)

R.No.79 - Bronze coiled finger ring, very thick and heavy, having four coils, greenish in colour, free ends tapering, made of a thick wire which slowly thins towards free ends; cross-section of the coil is round. From Period VI. Outer diameter is 2.20 cm., thickness in the centre is 0.40 cm., height is 1.80 cm. SKT-1, A1, Qd.1 (Pl.XLVI-4). Might have been used for toes of the feet.

R. No. 45 - Bronze coiled finger ring with four coils, squarish cross-section of the coil, corroded. Maximum outer diameter is 2.30 cm., thickness of wire of the coil is 0.30 cm., height is 1.3 cm., From Period VII. SKT 1, A1, Qd. 4. (Pl.XLVI-2)

C Bronze plates

Along with other antiquities, very thin, shallow, medium sized bronze plates with featureless rims were recovered from inside the burial jars. All are having raised convex shape in the middle. They are so paper thin that not a single one was recovered intact. They were found in highly corroded state. These plates occur in burials belonging to Periods IV, V and VI. Before and after these periods they are conspicuously absent. These bronze plates were not interned in all cases. Probably only the well to do families could spare bronze plates for the departed souls. Four were from Period IV, one from Period V and five from Period VI. These plates, as per their size, were probably offering plates to observe some ritual.

R. No. 336 - Papery thin plate, very shallow, almost flat with featureless straight margin with a circular ridge at the junction of margin and body. Diameter is 8.00 cm. From Period IV, SKT-1, A1, Qd.3. (Pl.XLVI-11)

R.No.285 - Bronze plate slightly thicker and bigger than No.336, surface polished for use. Diameter is 13.5 cm. From Period IV. SKT-1, A1, Qd.4. (Pl.XLVI-9)

R.No. 272 - Bronze plate, fortunately almost complete, very fragile, shallow, thin with featureless straight sharp rim, circular ridge between the junction of body and rim, i.e. at the neck region. Diameter is 9.5 cm. From Period VI. SKT-1, A1, Qd.3. (PlXL.VI-10)

R.No.304 - Same as above but with a very mild ridge. From Period V. Diameter is 11.00 cm. SKT-1, A1, Qd.2.

R. No. 335 - Same as No.336, diameter is 7.5 cm. From Period IV. SKT-1, A1, Qd.3.

D. Bronze *Ghungroos* (Trinklets)

Bells are known from the Megalithic burials at Hunur, Junapani, Mahurjhari and Khapa. The one of copper found in one of the pot burials at Hunur,[1] Distt. Belgaum has a rectangular base and a suspension loop at the top. Copper bells with iron tongue have been found at Junapani[2] and Mahurjhari[3]. Bells of iron, bronze/copper and silver are reported from Taxilla.

Small copper bells have been found in levels datable between *c.* 4th and 3rd centuries B.C. of Tumain. A small copper bell with an excurved rounded rim and a rectangular hole on the upper part is reported from Nagara. The copper bells with beaded loops at the top were found at Nevasa[4] in the 1st Century B.C. to 2nd--3rd century A.D. levels.

In all nine *Ghungroos* (trinklets) were recovered from the burials. Six belong to Period VI, two to Period V and one to Period IV. No *Ghungroo* was recovered from the last period. All are made of bronze or bell-metal.

Five are decorated while the rest are plain. Five have two petals and four are with four petals. Each is having an almost circular ring at the top to facilitate fastening in a thread or in an iron rod (as found in one case). From some a small pebble was recovered which is put inside the trinklet for emitting sound.

---

1. *Indian Archaeology 1968-69-A Review*, pp.20-21.
2. *Indian Archaeology 1961-62-A Review*, p. 32.
3. Deoia, S.B., *Mahurjhari Excavation*, 1970-72, 1973.
4. Sankalia, H.D., S.B. Deo, Ansari, Z.D. and Ehrdt's *From History to Prehistory at Nevasa* (1954-56).

R.No.226 - A medium size *Ghungroo* of bell-metal having four petals. Just above the petals a ridge runs horizontally around the body, followed by another on top where the circular suspension loop has been luted. From Period IV, diameter of the bud portion is 2.90 cm., diameter of the suspension loop is 1.60 cm. Length is 2.80 cm., SKT-1, A1, Qd.2. (PL.XXX-5)

R.No.293 - A complete medium sized *Ghungroo* of bell-metal. Slightly larger than No.226, having four petals. Just above the petal line a thick ridge (thickness 0.30 cm.) runs around the body, whereas another one of the same thickness runs on the top. Both are decorated with vertical incised lines. The bell is topped by a circular suspension loop luted to the body of the bell. From Period V. Maximum length is 4.50 cm. Maximum diameter in the central part is 2.20 cm. Diameter of suspension loop is 1.20 cm. SKT-1, A1, Qd.1. (Pl.XXX-2).

R.No.174 - A medium sized bell-metal bell with four petals. Broken, plain. Inside the circular suspension loop an iron circular ring is inserted. It appears that a number of trinklets were suspended from an iron ring. Maximum length is 3.00 cm., diameter of bell part is 1.70 cm., diameter of suspension loop is 1.40 cm. From Period V. SKT-1, A1, Qd.2. (Pl.XXX-6).

R.No.72 - Well polished, greenish bell metal *Ghungroo* of bigger size having two petals and a circular suspension loop luted to the body on top. The petals have been decorated with wavy incised lines running in receding order from the free ends of the petals to the top. From Period VI. Height of bell including handle is 3.70 cm., width of the petal is 3-10 cm. diameter of suspension loop is 1.30 cm. SKT-1, A1, Qd.1. (Pl.XXX-1).

R.No.76 - A two petalled round greenish well polished bell-metal *Ghungroo*, both petals decorated with concentric incised thin lines. The heart shaped suspension loop with a long bar is luted to the top of the bell body. Broken. From Period VI. Height is 4.70 cm., diameter of the petal part is 2.40 cm., length of suspension loop is 2.30 cm. SKT-1, A1, Qd.1. (Pl.XXX-3).

R.No.94 - Same as No.76, but with more deep concentric lines. Broken into pieces. From Period VI. Length is 4.50 cm, width is 2.70 cm, length of handle is 2.00 cm., the hole of suspension loop is double convex. SKT-1,A1, Qd.2. (Pl.XXX-4).

R.No.131 - A medium sized, round bell-metal *Ghungroo* with four petals, plain having two ridges at the top. A circular suspension loop is luted to the body, heavily corroded. From Period VI. Height is 2.40 cm., diameter of body is 1.70 cm, diameter of suspension loop is 0.90 cm. SKT-1, A1, Qd.2. (Pl.XXX-7).

R.No.277 - A miniature variety of No.76. Complete with a circular suspension loop. From Period VI. Height is 1.85 cm., width is 1.20 cm., diameter of suspension loop is 0.70 cm. SKT-1, A1, Q.3. (Pl.XXX-8).

R.No.378 - Same as No.277, but in fragments. From Period VI. SKT-1, A1, Qd.3.

E. Bronze Pots

R.No.56 - Bronze bowl with a pedestal base, has a slightly everted internally bevelled rim and slightly bulging, fragile. Waist region is decorated with four horizontal grooves externally. From Period VI, found along with bracelets, bangles and beads inside big jar. Height is 4.50 cm., diameter of rim is 8.00 cm., diameter of base is 5.1 cm. SKT-1,A1,Qd.4. (Pl.XLVII-A).

R.No.313 - Bronze flower vase with a pedestal base having triangular perforated designs. It has a long funnel shaped neck with straight, everted featureless rim. At the neck region there is carination in the form of a horizontal ridge, belly portion is bulbous with the broadest portion suddenly ending into a cylindrical stem attached to the flaring, decorated wide base. From Period V. This base was found offered to a copper masked human skull both kept inside a big jar. Height is 13.30 cm., diameter of rim is 5.80 cm., diameter of belly is 6.3 cm., diameter of base is 6.40 cm. SKT-1, A1, Qd.4. (Pl.XLVII-B).

R.No.316 - Bronze casket (relic) from Period V. A typical Buddhist relic casket, with a cylindrical body, wide flaring hollow pedestal base. Body and base joined by a narrow cylindrical waist. The lid's lower part which fits in the body of main pot is cylindrical while the upper part is crowned by a thin three tiered crown topped by a pyramidal head with a square base. The upper part of the lid is typical of a *Chatravali* over the *hermika* of a stupa. As the casket is broken at the base of the cylindrical body, bone relics that might have been put inside the casket were found missing. The casket was recovered from a big jar along with beads. Height of the casket is 23.00 cm., diameter of cylindrical body is 6.20 cm., diameter of base is 7.80 cm., height of *Chatravali* is 4.20 cm., distance between each line is 0.60 cm., height of crown is 1.50 cm. SKT-1, A1, Qd.1 (Pl XXIXA).

F. Copper Masks (Pls. XXIIIA, XXVII, XXIXB and XLVIII)

Masks used as coverings for the face either as a protective screen or disguise have not been found at any site. Representations of masked human figures are found on paintings in rock-shelters which have been dated variously between the Mesolithic and the historical periods.

In Sekta burials, all the human skulls recovered from the pots had copper masks over them. Such skulls were interned in the later periods, i.e. from Period

V to VII. The masks were moulded out of very thin sheets of copper, carefully delineating the facial parts. Eyes had been shown in the form of two bulging out dots. It is evident that the human skulls were covered with the masks only during the second internment of the skull inside the earthern pot along with other funerary offerings.

With respect to the discovery of masked human skulls Manipur occupies an unique position in the country as, so far, such masked skulls have not been reported from any site. With the discovery of masked skulls from the excavations at Sekta, the doubts lurking in the minds of scholars about the antiquity of gold masked skulls recovered from a hillock named Lambui Ching Chingmeirong in Imphal town in 1980 and a similar skull recovered in bronze casket, from the slopes of Thumkhong Ching hills near Sekta on 4.9.1989 have been cleared. The excavation finds show that the above mentioned finds from the hill slopes are not of recent origin and the unique ritual practice of covering the skulls with masks, gold or copper, depending on the economic and social status of the deceased, is an exclusive ritual which was being practised in Manipur during the beginning of the Christian era.

C. Coin

A heavily corroded copper coin was recovered from Trench A1, Qd.4 at the depth of 40.0 cms. from Period VI. Its dimensions are 2.20 x 2.10 x 0.20 cm. The legends could not be read as they are in highly corroded condition.

D. Beads (Pl-XLIX to LIII, Fig. 22)

From inside the burial pots a large number of beads of different sizes and in different colours made out of paste, glass and semi-precious stones were recovered. The number of beads particularly micro ones is so large in each burial that it is difficult to count. Paste beads were numerically conspicuous. It appears that the people of Sekta right from Period II onwards were very much fond of beads of all shapes and sizes. Beads were available in plenty. This shows that the people loved wearing ornaments. It is difficult to say whether there was a bead factory in the area, i.e. in Manipur valley, where they were being manufactured or only paste and glass beads were locally made and beads of semi-precious stones were being imported into the valley from other areas. The occurrence of particularly carnelian beads clearly shows that there was regular contact with the Indo-Gangetic plains of the country right upto Kutch where, from Harappan times onwards, manufacture of carnelian beads was an industry. Paste beads start occurring from Period II onwards whereas glass beads make their appearance from Period III onwards. Beads were interned inside the pots along with other grave goods like bangles, rings, iron objects and fragmentary human bones. Generally beads were found in association with human teeth (molars and premolars) which also looked like beads.

Dikshit[1] writes, "the word bead is derived from the Saxon verb "bidden" to pray and was originally associated with the "beads" on a rosary. But it now means almost any pierced object which can be strung. Beads are particularly valuable for an archaeologist because they are unrivalled in tracing the influence of one culture on another, of one race or nation on another, especially in ancient times. This is because of "their great diversity of form, portability and lasting power".

R.No.334 - A terracotta large bead which might have been used as a pendant, grey in colour, bulbous, barrel shaped with large hole, decorated in the centre and at two ends, with granulated design. From Period IV. Horizontal length is 4.60 cm., diameter in the centre is 5.60 cm., diameter of thread hole is 1.70 cm. SKT-1, A1, Qd.3 (Pl.XLIX-A-2).

R.No.203 - A stone pendant, triangular of Himalayan schist, hole at the top end. From Period V, length is 2.90 cm., width is 2.40 cm. SKT-1, A1, Qd.1.(Pl.XLIXA-1).

Glass Beads

A large number of glass beads in various sizes and shapes and colours were found from different levels right from Period III above. They are generally of opaque variety with shades of green, blue, blue-green, red, brown, yellowish, white and dull white. They occur in the following shapes - spherical, spheroid, short-truncated bi-cone circular, cylindrical circular, bevel shaped, lenticular, short cylindrical, circular with gadroons, etc. The spherical and cylindrical are the most common ones. Their sizes vary from 6 mm to micro ones.

Sravasti, Kausambi, Patliputra, Maheswar, Kopia, Ahicchatra, Rajghat, Tripuri and several other sites have given abundant evidence of glass beads of various types and techniques. By the beginning of the Christian era the use of glass beads became quite common.

Faience and paste beads are most numerous. They are mostly white in colour. Faience is a term originally applied to a material made in the town of Faenza. It is a product consisting of fine powdered quartz mixed with a small quantity of some other material to act as a flux and then fired.

A few beads of carnelian have also been recovered. This was a favourite material for bead making in ancient India. The principal source of the material was the large deposit near Ratnapur in Gujarat. An extensive bead industry exists near Cambay from ancient times. A typical octagonal barrel shaped carnelian bead with a deep circular groove was picked up from A1, Qd.4 at the depth of 4.0 cm. from Period VII.

1. Dikshit, M.G., *Some Beads from Kondapur,* Hyderabad, Archaeological Series No. 18, 1952

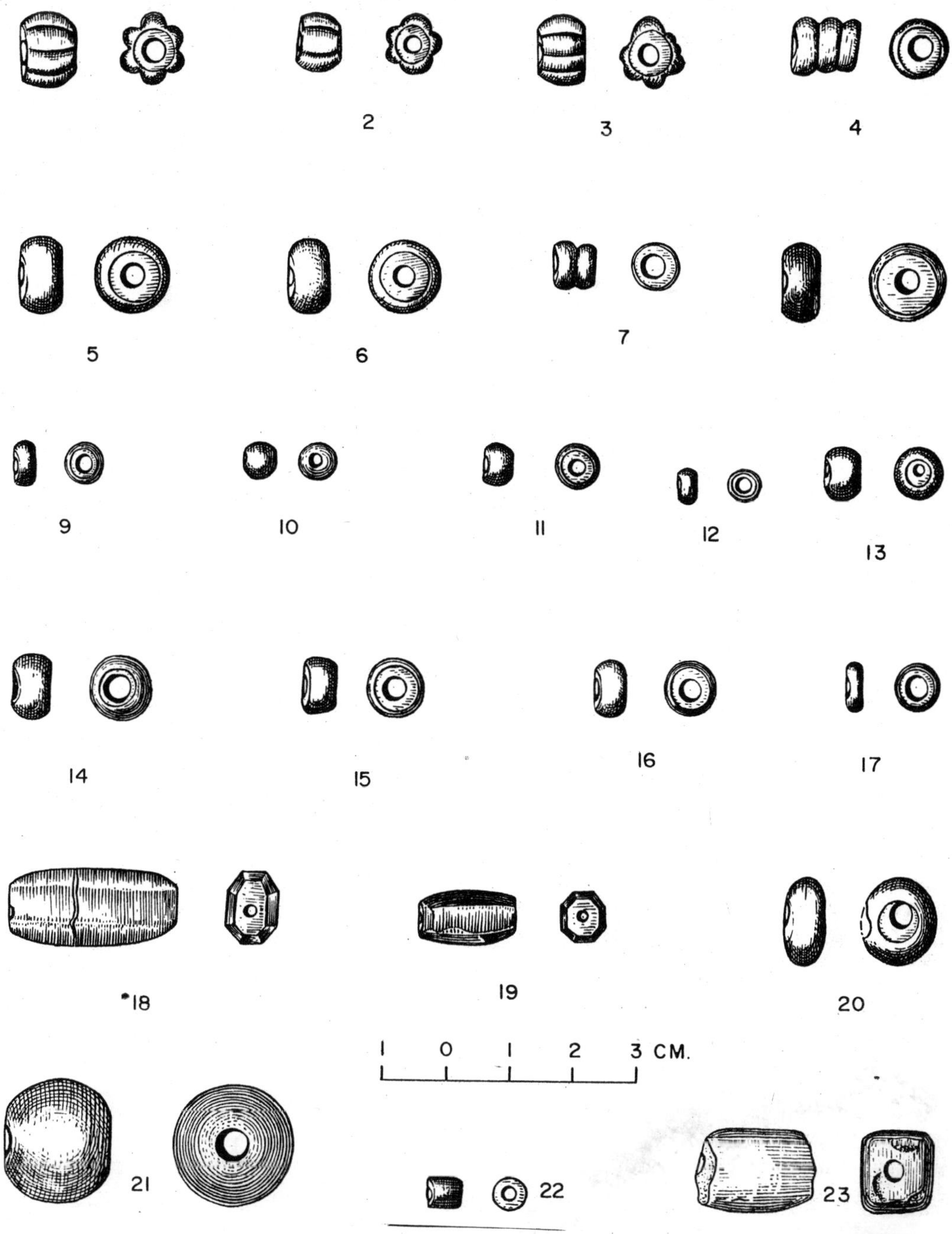

Fig. 22

The beads recovered from Sekta burials could be variously dated but it is certain that the paste beads made their appearance around 200 to 300 B.C. whereas glass beads probably a century or two later.As already stated earlier, by the beginning of the Christian era the use of glass bead became very common so there is nothing unusual in Sekta burials having a large number of glass beads.

Fig. 22

No.1. It is a large bead of the melon type cut from a long tube. It has gadroons all over the body. Opaque white glass. Such beads have been found in large numbers from Satavahana levels of different sites. From Period IV.

No.2. A shorter variety of above on opaque colourless glass. From Period V.

No.3. A medium sized melon bead of paste with deep gadroons. From Period III.

No.4. A segmented paste bead whitish in colour. The ends show that it was prepared out of long cones by blowing. They are not very frequent. This one is having three segments. No.7 is a smaller variety of the above with only two segments. From Period IV.

No.5. Globular bead of paste, white in colour. This is a very common shape and a large number of beads are of this type. From Period III.

No.6. Globular bead of glass, green in colour.

No.7 to 17 All globular beads of different sizes in glass and paste, while those in paste are white, glass ones are green, brown and dull red in colour. From Period V.

No.18. An octagonal carnelian barrel bead. Carnelian is not of very good red variety. It has a deep circular groove over the body. From Period VI.

No.19. An octagonal barrel bead made of banded agate. It has been carefully polished. Period VI.

No.20 Globular bead of bluish glass, large in size. Period V.

No.21. Globular bead of terracotta from Period VI.

No.22. A cylindrical bead of green glass from Period V.

No.23. Standard, truncated biconal, square faceted, dirty white glass bead from Period VII.

E. Miscellaneous objects

An incised scale

The evidence of Sekta people having knowledge of linear measurements is found from the recovery of incised linear divisions on a potsherd. Each division is equal and measures 0.70 cm. (Pl.XXX VII A)

Terracotta marble - R.No. 205 - Period VI, SKT-1, A1, Qd2.

7. Conclusions

The limited dig has revealed a lot of information about the burial customs of Sekta people, their social and economic life hitherto not known. The excavation has also cleared many unfounded misgivings that prevailed among the historians of Manipur.

Shrinking of the lakes in Manipur valley, the last phase of which happened some time during 7000 B.C., and stripping of hill slopes led to weakening of south-west monsoon and comparatively intensified winter monsoon. After the shrinking of the lakes the drainage patterns that emerged led to the formation of Imphal, Iril and other river systems in the valley. All these rivers and their tributaries normally flow from north to south. These rivers are still cutting deep into the sand, silt and clay deposits of the valley as could be ascertained from the study of the Iril River near Sekta.

The evidence shows that much after silting of the lakes, which exposed a large flat fertile area and much after formation of the Iril River system people settled at Sekta right on the virgin soil which is yellowish compact clay.

Presence of at least six burial mounds in Sekta indicates that it was a fairly large settlement with sizeable population.

Recovery of large number of handmade and wheel made pottery with numerous designs, shapes and sizes and good quantity of antiquities from each burial is indicative of the fact that people were economically prosperous. The well laid urn burials right from the bottom to the top shows that Sekta had a well organised society practising meticulously the social norms and customs established by the people. Iron armaments in the burials point out that these were designed for defensive purposes against the enemies of the deceased. Their presence suggests the warrior qualities of Manipuris, constantly threatened by sudden attacks. Placement of arms in the burials became part of the burial practice.

Recovery of copper, brass and iron objects show that they had knowledge of metallurgy of these metals. In fact during our exploration of the eastern hills bordering Burma, we came across large deposits of iron ore some 15 kms. west of Moreh and copper deposits near Ukhrul.

It appears that people of Sekta were making pottery locally. Bulk of the pottery recovered is handmade with several designs and shapes. Several patterns of mat designs, cord impressions, fish bone impressions, tortoise shell impressions, punched designs, stamped designs, etc. are available. Pots are mostly jars, bowls, platters, vases and dishes with straight and flaring rims. Red ware, grey ware and partly black and red ware have been encountered. Over the handmade pots a very thin slip that gets dissolved in water and makes the pot look ochorous have been applied. Wheel made pottery recovered from lower levels is generally thin, fine slipped red ware and have been prepared from well levigated clay and well fired.

Recovery of wheel made pottery both from the habitation and burial areas has finally dispelled the so far held view that wheel made pottery was not known to Manipur. This is an important contribution.

Presence of atleast six burial mounds indicates that there were either more than one sect of people living in Sekta who had their own separate burial area or possibly the society was divided into different strata, may be on occupational basis, who had their own burial grounds. But this needs to be verified by excavating atleast 2 to 3 more burial mounds in the area.

There is total absence of animal bones in the urns.

Recovery of a large number of beads of semi-precious stones, glass, terracotta, etc. indicate that Manipur had regular contact with other parts of the Indian sub-continent, particularly with the western side. As none of the bone fragments show any burning mark, it appears that after the death of the deceased, the body was either buried or exposed to open air and fragments of important bones were later collected and deposited inside the urns. The urn burials at Sekta show remarkable similarity with the urn burials excavated from other parts of India, particularly from south and south-east India. It is certain that there is absolutely no Burmese influence in the burial customs of Manipur during the period under study. The practice of secondary burial, preceded by a process of excarnation is a widely practised system in the Indian sub-continent right from Neolithic times onwards. Mundas[1] and Nicobarese[2] still practise the system of re-burial. These similar features are probably manifestations of a common spiritual heritage, notwithstanding their differences in the sphere of material culture.

---

1. Roy, S.C. *The Mundas and their country*, Ranchi, 1912.
2. Sewell, R. and B.S. Guha, *Human Remains from cemetery at Nal, South Baluchistan.*

The burials which contained objects like weapons for defence such as spear head, daggers, etc. or *chillum* normally did not contain copper bangles and vice versa. This is indicative of male and female burial practices.

The very limited dig in the habitation area revealed a house floor made up of yellow compact clay. In the floor atleast two post poles were clearly visible. This shows that the houses were built on bamboo or wooden poles and were covered on sides with mats plastered with wattle and daub as is the present practice. (Pl.VIIA).

On the basis of comparative study of iron objects from Sekta with those from sites like Tripuri, Nagda, etc. Period VI and VII of Sekta could be of similar date as that of stratum V of Tripuri which has been dated from A.D. A.D. 200-400. Objects from Period V of Sekta are comparable to those from Stratum IV of Tripuri and Period III of Ujjain which have been dated to 100 B.C. - to A.D. 200 and 600 B.C. to 200 B.C. respectively. Period III, II and I at Sekta will thus definitely be of much earlier dates.

The pot burials with copper and bronze objects interned in them along with human skeletal remains could be compared to such pot burials excavated at Khuntitoli, District Ranchi in Bihar by Dr.S.C.Ray[1]. At Khuntitoli the grave goods consisted of a central urn with lid placed in a special depression. The burials contained a few beads of agate, coral, red paste, copper and bronze, a copper-bronze bangle and few bronze rings. No iron on any datable object was obtained from these burials. They have been dated to the beginning of the Christian era. (Pl.LV).

On a conservative estimate the beginning of habitation, i.e. Period I at Sekta, on the left bank of Iril, could be easily assigned to the later half of the first millennium B.C. if not earlier. This is subject to support by absolute dating for which results of the material sent to the Physical Research laboratory, Ahmedabad are still awaited.

The evidence of prevalance of Buddhism in the valley is available at Sekta in the form of a bronze relic casket from Period V. As this period could be dated to 100 B.C. to A.D. 200 it appears that this religion reached Manipur valley around the beginning of the Christian era or even a little earlier. The find at Sekta is not an isolated evidence, an exactly similar casket made of silver along with other antiquities like a silver hollow horse with a long narrow spout emerging from below the neck region and passing beyond the mouth and a *chatri* resting over a cylindrical stand which in turn was planted on the back of the horse, (Pl.IX) a gold masked human skull and a piece of

1. Indian Archaeology-1965-66-a Review.

a handle of fly-whisk made of silver were recovered from a hillock named Lambui Ching Chingmeirang in Imphal town in 1980 during levelling operations of the area. The gold mask was further decorated with a silver belt, semi-precious stone and coral beads (Pl.VIIB). Apart from these evidences bronze and stone statues' of Buddha and Bodhisattva have been found from Kakching, Chandel and Leuthabal. The statues could now be seen in the State Museum at Imphal. (Pl.LVI A&B)

It appears from these archaeological evidences that Manipur was also swayed by the wave of Buddhism much earlier, say around the beginning of the Christian era, when this religion was spreading towards east. Due to some reason or the other it could not make a very deep impact on the life of the people in Manipur and that is why, so far, no archaeological evidences in the form of Buddhist monasteries, viharas and stupas have come to light. Of course, it could be argued that this lacuna may be partly due to the absence of detailed explorations in Manipur, particularly in the 'U' shaped valleys as such valleys were generally liked by the Buddhists for the establishments of monasteries and viharas.

The question now posed before us is as to who were the authors of this urn burial civilization and from where did they come from or with which area they had regular contacts ?

The discovery of a large number of Neoliths (Pl.IIIA) and Megaliths (Pl.X) in Manipur led Choudhury (1959) to postulate, "to whatever people the stone celts belonged, whether the Mon-khmers of the Austric stock or others, they show definite links not only with Burma, Malaya and Oceanic world but also with central and southern India and with the Gangetic valley and the west". One view based on some anthropometric data which shows presence of some Veddoid strain in eastern India, is that a group of Veddoids came to this area before the arrival of the Mongoloids.

The excavations at Sekta now clearly demonstate that during early historical times, i.e. around the later half of 1st millennium B.C., Manipur had close cultural relations with central and adjoining eastern India. Though the present population of Manipur is predominantly Mongoloid in facial character, it has been observed that there is also the presence of dolicocephalic head, facial - prognethism, alveolar-prognethism, thickened lip, very low, wavy or curly head hair and developed supra-orbital ridges. It appears that the Mongoloid tribes came in contact with the long headed people from the west, i.e. plains of India when the latter reached the area via the Surma and Brahmaputra valleys in search of fresh lands (Das 1967, Barkataki 1967). In course of time, particularly in the valleys, the culture brought by people coming from the west became dominant.

Moreover, as the hill ranges in the western side of Manipur are lower than their eastern counterparts, it was but natural for people from western side to establish contacts with the very fertile land and receptive people of Manipur than those from the east. Discovery of a number of sites belonging to early historical period, particularly yielding urn burials, along the two banks of River Iril, point out towards their origin and affinity with Gangetic plain, Bihar, Bengal and Southern India where urn burial practices were quite predominant during the first millennium B.C.

Excavations at Sekta has contributed immensely to the early history of India in general and Manipur in particular. There are certain evidences like masking of human skulls before second internment, which have come to light for the first time in the country and it speaks about the strange religio-social custom of the people in Manipur during the beginning of the Christian era. Continuation of the handmade pottery traditions with exactly the same decorations and designs that originated in Neolithic times in Manipur and in other parts of the country, speaks of continuity of cultural traditions for millenniums. This is again unique to Manipur.

Further investigation in this archaeologically rich area will reveal many unknown facts and dispel wrong notions based on flimsy evidences and put the history of Manipur in correct perspective.

Before closing it will be worthwhile to reproduce the speech of Dr. Y. Mohendra Singh, Principal, C.I. College, Bishnupur delivered during the opening of Sekta exhibition at Imphal.

"The antiquity of 'SEKTA' is found mentioned in the 'THANGMEIROL', a chronicle which deals with the politico-geography of THANGMEI MAR. (Page 14 of my *Thangemeirol* in archaic script). Thangwai Mar is one of the venerated ancestors of the Manipuris. The reason why the place has been called 'SEKTA' was that when THANGWAI MAR caught the wigned horse SANATON AYANGBA, the place had the shadow of the horse (SEKTA-SHEK: Shadow: TA - TO HIT). The place has since been called SEKTA. According to the "THANGMEIROL", THANGWAI MAR settled in the LANGMEI range and that THANGMEI MAR taught the principles of administration before POIREITON introduced the same. This reference in the Thangemeirol shows that Thangemeirol was earlier than Poireiton. Poireton was contemporarneous to NONGDA LAIREL PAKHANGBA who is regarded to have become king in A.D. 33 or 3135 years in KALI AGE, according to *Cheitharol Kumbaba* and other chronicles. In early times, YUDHISTIR ERA was prevalent in North-Eastern India. Thangmei Mar was, therefore, earlier than Nongda. The Manipuris have still SAMATON AYANGBA as their cultural symbol. The winged horse captured by Thangwai Mar needs to be examined. In this context it is to be noted that the Ahom Tais have horse as their cultural symbol. The Tai people have horse as their companion.

In this connection it is of great interest to note that Nongda Lairen Pakhangba was immediately preceded by the Pongs according to *Shingkak,* a chronicle which gives a list of kings chronologically. The Manipuris call Man as the Pong and European scholars define Pong as Mao-Shan, a branch of the Great Tai Race. There are references in the local chronicles to the statement that the Angoms, one of the important clans of the Manipuris were born of the Pongs. And Nongda Lairen Pakhangba who was the progenitor of the Meities class (NINGTHOUJA) was the younger brother of Poireiton, the progenitor of the Angoms. KONJIL TUTHOKPA, the first Pakhangba of the 'Creation' had given birth to the Pong king. In another chronicle Soralel gave birth to KHUNLU who had become Pong King. There are chronicles which refer to POIREITON as KABO Poireiton. This reference becomes significant when we know that the CHAKPTAS, a scheduled caste Manipuris, came from Kabo Valley (Upper Burma). The CHAKPAS preceded NONGDA LAIREN PAKHANGBA.

The upper head of the Iril River was also known as the MEERA-PONG-THOKLAM, i.e. the place from where the Pongs came out.

Of the findings at the Sekta mound pottery dominates. When Manipuris talk of pottery, the CHAKPAS cannot escape from our notice easily. The chronicles and the present existing tradition prove without any controversy that the CHAKPAS have been the manufacturers of pottery since time immemorial in Manipur. The present pottery made by the Chakpas bears 'NOORA KONDO LEI', a kind of flower: This is also a cultural symbol of the Manipuris. Had there not been plenty of pottery, the remains of the dead body should not have been put inside the pottery for burial. The inhabitants of Sekta must have had plenty of pottery and therefore my observation is that the inhabitants should be manufacturers of pottery. The means of communications available at the disposal of the inhabitants of Sekta in those days should have prevented import of pottery from other places.

The preservation of the skull of the dead body is a cultural trait of the TAI people. Ahok Tai people preserved the skulls of the dead. The *Sakok Lamlem* and other chronicles describe the manner of preservation of the skulls. The burial site at Sekta proves that inhabitants did not burn their dead bodies. The site therefore presents pre-Hindu culture. This is further strengthened by the Buddhist casket found in the burial site. In this connection it is also interesting to note that the 'PAKHANGBA LAILING' the so-called Pakhangba

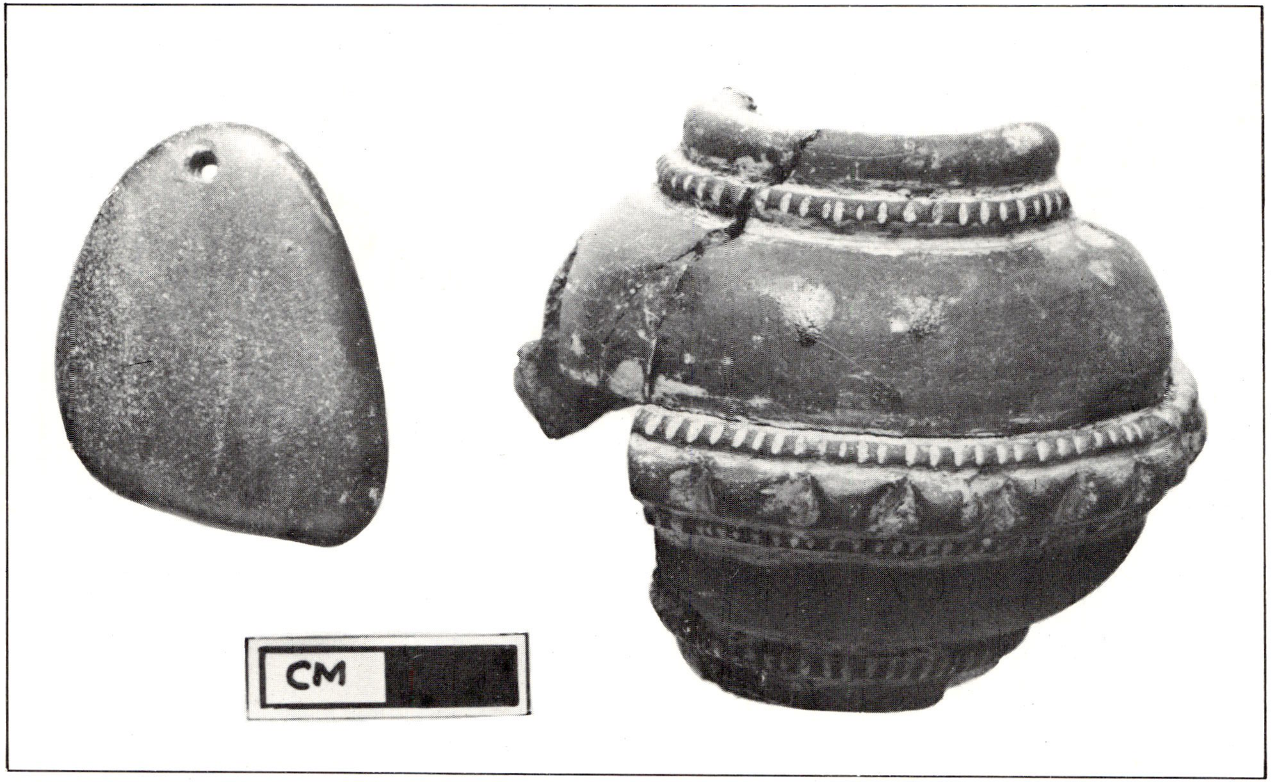

XLIX. Beads.

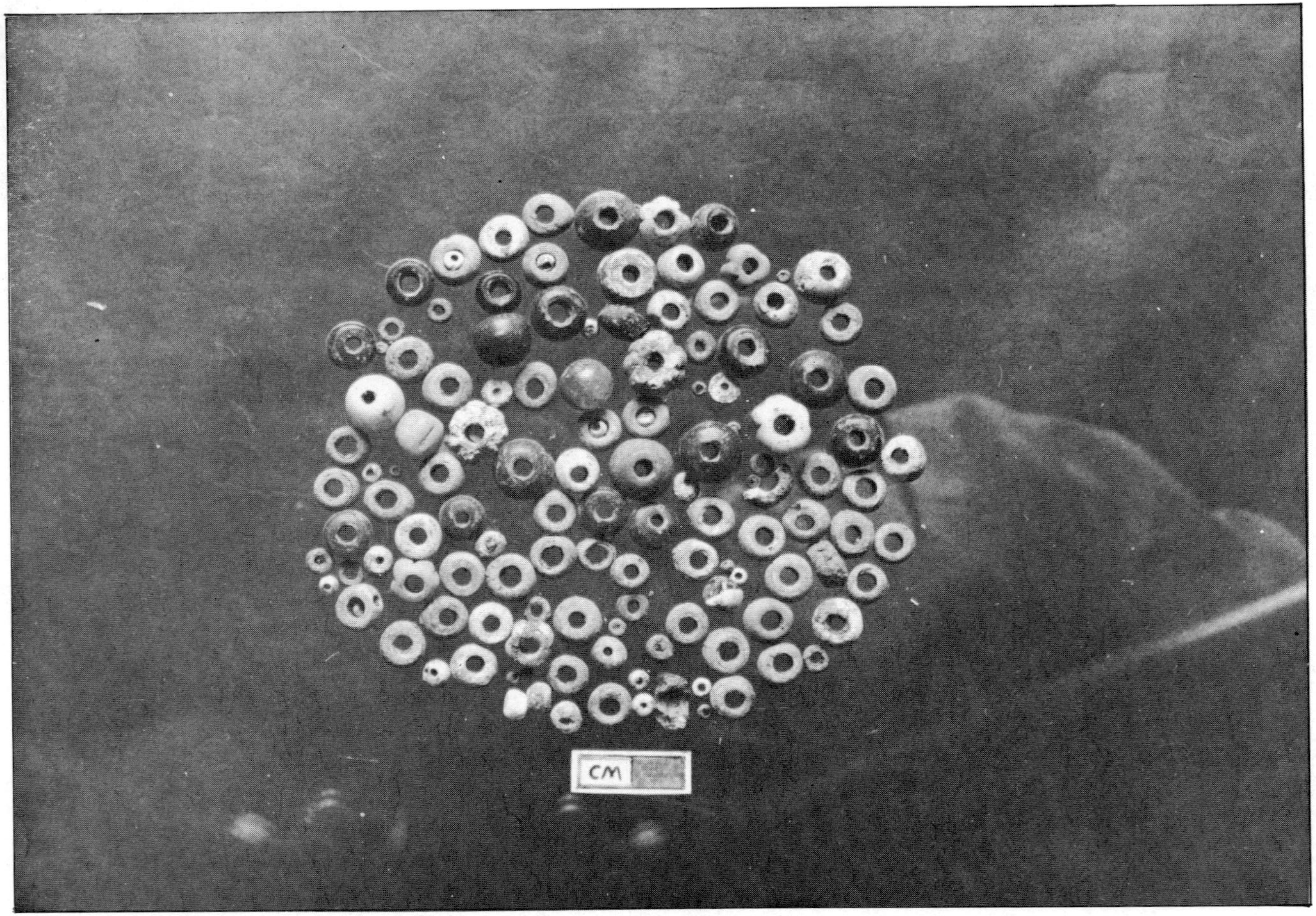

L. Beads.

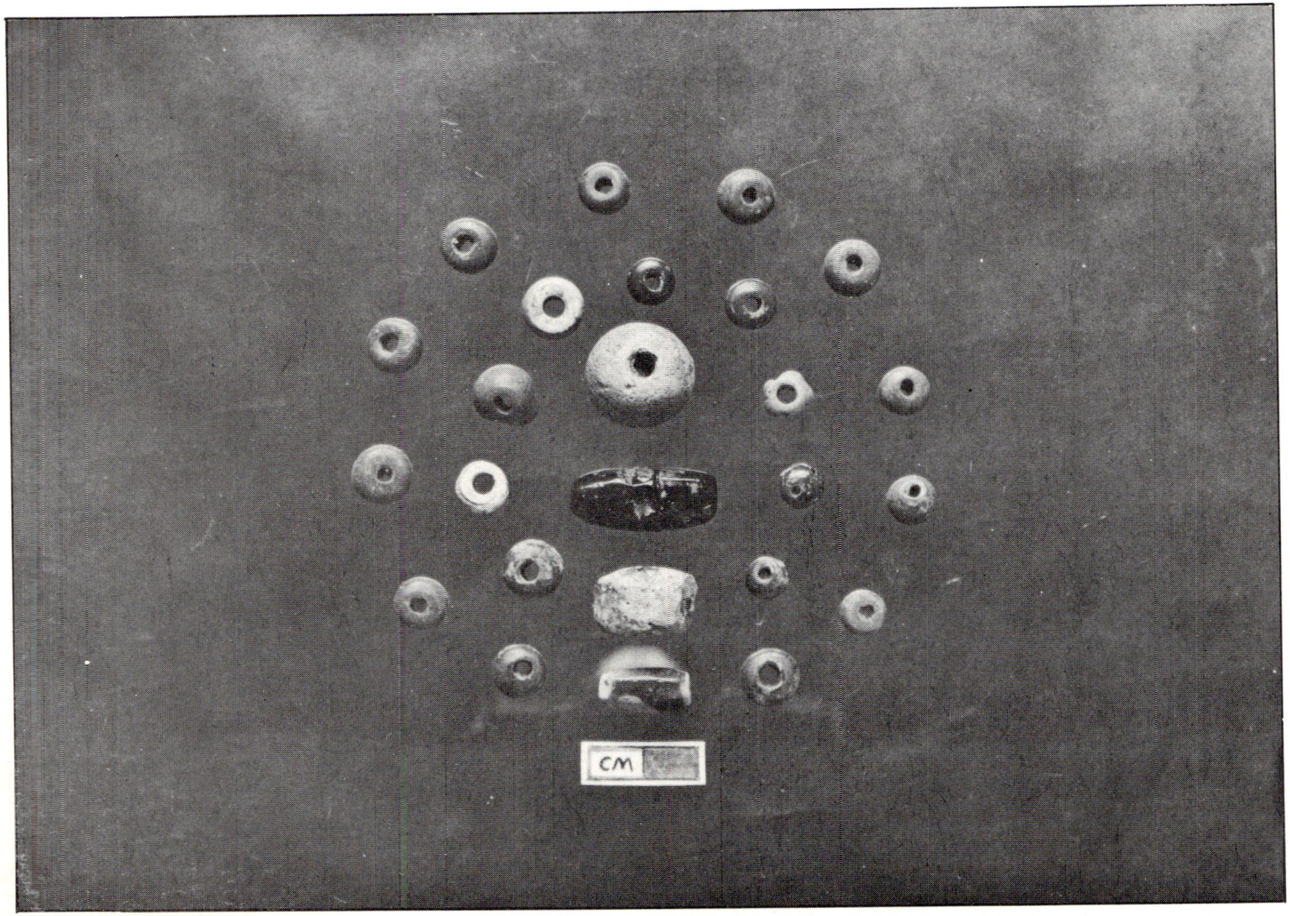

LI. Beads.

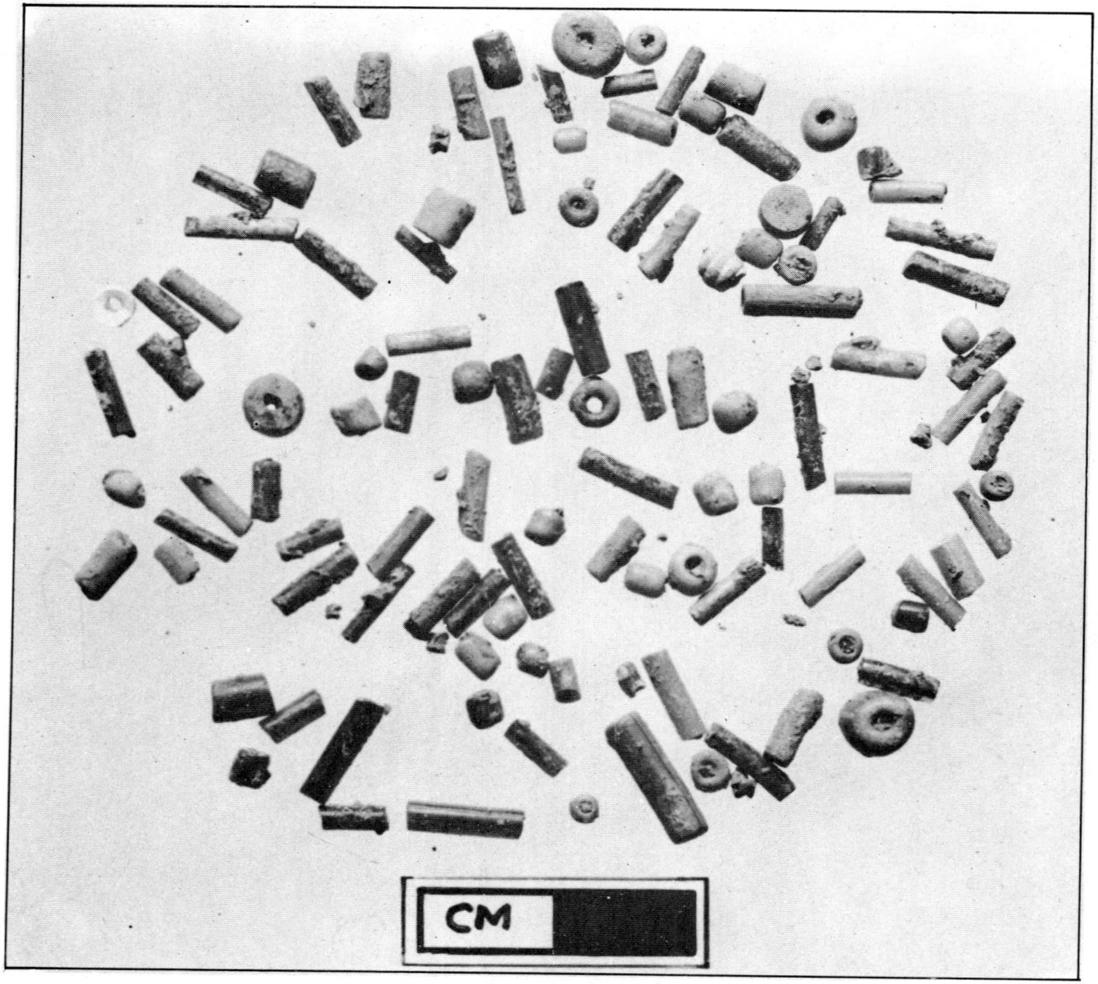

LII. Beads.

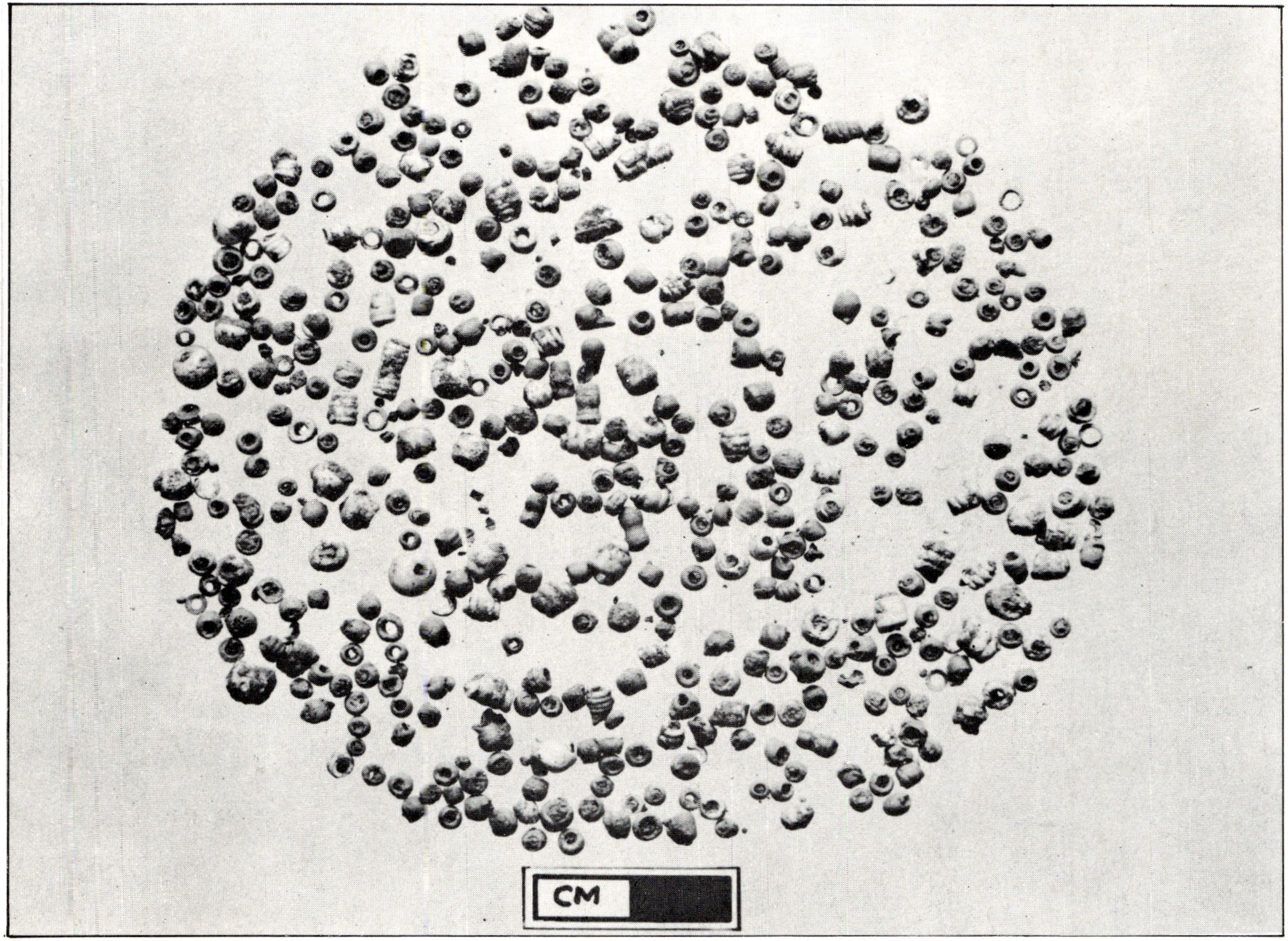

LIII. Beads.

LIV. Floor level in habitation area along with post-holes.

LV. Pot burials from Khuntitoli, Bihar.

LVI. A & B. Seated Buddha.

religion contains non-injury as one of its tenets. This is called in the local vocabulary as YAIBI-THAWAI NGAKPA - preservation of life; not to destroy the life. Hence non-injury.

Of the coin having the word 'Rama' it is also interesting to note that Manipur was surrounded by the Hindu kingdoms in the pre-Christian era. Kamarupa or Pragyajotishpur (Assam) on the west, the PYUS (The Priya) on the east (Burma), Chittagong and Yunan. Further Manipur is on the fringe of South-East Asia mainland on the west.

The early history of the South-East Asia shows how the Indian culture exercised a tremendous influence on the culture and civilisation of the indigenous people of South-East Asia. The most unique contribution is the introduction of the art of writing as KA, KHA, GA, etc. amongst the peoples of South-East Asian countries. Even Manipur was a part of Assam in early period. The identification of the coin should be on the background of this cultural scenario.

Another point which needs our attention is the influence of Chinese culture on those people of the South-East Asian countries. However, the Chinese influence was lesser than that of the Indian culture. The people of Manipur should have also felt the Chinese influence.

Lastly, the findings from the Sekta Mound excavation shall certainly serve as the turning point in the early history of Manipur.

The last very important question which needs to be discussed is regarding the geneology of kings of Manipur which starts with Paakhangba (Yubishta) in A.D. 33 and ends with Bodha Chandra in A.D. 1949. This geneology has been doubted by a section of scholars in Manipur due to lack of supporting archaeological evidences. They have termed it to be a fake one, deliberately got prepared by the later kings to establish their relationship and descendency with respectable ruling classes in the Indo-Gangetic plains.

In India keeping alive the geneology of families is a very ancient tradition which travelled orally from generation to generation. These geneologies, both, of the important families and commoners, were preserved by Pandas of Prayag, Kashi and Gaya, the three most important centres concerning the last journey of Hindus. Normally no one would like to tamper with these and that too the ruling class which was more conscious of their lineage.

Now in the light of the evidences unearthed at Sekta, where atleast seven periods of burials have been identified, the kings geneology needs to be considered carefully as even on the basis of dates based on pottery and antiquity, the time of the first king in the list, Paakhangba (A.D. 33) nearly coincides, atleast, with the second phase of handmade pottery era, if not earlier. It was this period from where the profusion of offering beads and other ornaments alongwith weapons of iron, a definite sign of prosperity, start occurring in the burials. The third king in the list. Taothing Maang also named as Talagatya. who is supposed to have ruled around the middle of second century A.D. is significant, as the velic casket unearthed falls around this time bracket indicating that Buddhism seems to have made some inroad around this period in Manipur.

I do not wish to state that these arguments authenticate the geneology but would like to emphasise that the evidences of Sekta may help in solving the problem. There is need to excavate a few more sites like Sekta in order to reach some firm conclusion. Sekta is the beginning in this direction and may prove to be a turning point so far as the archaeological evidences about the glorious past of Manipur is concerned.

Bibliography

Abdul Ali., *Notes on Early History of Manipur,* Calcutta, 1923

Acharyya, N.N., *Source Materials for the Early History and Culture of North-Eastern States of India:* A Historical Approach, Bulletin of the Assam State Museum, No.IV, 1982.

Unexplored Sources for the History of *Manipur,* Sources of History of India, Vol.IV., ed. N.R. Ray.

Acharyya, N.N., *Assam and Neighbouring States-Historical Documents,* New Delhi, 1983.

Acharyaa, N.N., *North-east as viewed by Foreigners,* New Delhi, 1984.

Agrawal, D.P., Kusumgar, S., and Sara, R.P., 'Radio Carbon dates of Archaeological samples', *Current Science,* vol.33, No.9, 1964.

Alemchiba, M., *A Brief Hisorical Account of Nagaland,* Kohina, 1970

Ali, A.F.M., "Manipur Through the Ages" in *Peeps in Manipur,* compiled by R.K. Sanapal, Imphal, 1985.

Allchin, B&R., *The Birth of Indian Civilization,* Penguin Books Ltd., Harmondsworth, Middlesex, England, 1968.

– Ancient India Nos.11 & 12.

Arkell, "Cambay and the Bead-Track", *Antiquity,* Vol.X

Banerjee, N.R., *Iron Age in India,* 1967.

Banerjee, N.R., *Nagda* 1955-57, New Delhi, 1986.

Bagchi, P.C., *India and China.*

Barkataki, S., Some aspects of tribal life in Assam. In *Kamarupa,* B.M. Das(Ed.), Gauhati. 1967.

Barua, K.L., *Early History of Kamarupa,* 1933.

Barron, Lt., Note on stone implements from the Naga Hills, *Jr. Royal Anth Inst.* I: 61-62. (Appendix). 1872.

Barua, B.K., *A cultural History of Assam,* Gauhati, (2nd Edn.) 1969.

Basak, R.G., *History of North Eastern India,* Calcutta, 1967.

Beal, S., *Travels of Yuwan Chwang*, London, 1888.

Bulletinde, I, 'Ecole Francaire De Extreme Orient, 1904.

Bulletein of Mutna Museum, *Coins of Manipur.* 1982.

Childe, V. Gordan., *New Light on the Most Ancient East*, London, 1954.

Choudhury, P.C., *The History of Civilization of People of Assam upto the 5th century A.D.*, Gauhati, 1959.

Choudhury, V. and Ray, P., *The Coinage of Manipur*, Vide Supra, No.6.

Choudhury, P.C., *Historical Archaeology of Central Assam* (from earliest time to 12th century A.D.), 1985.

Codrington, K.de B., 'Indian Cairn and Urn burials' in *Man*, XXX, 1930.

Codrington, K.de B., Indian Cairn and Urn Burials, *Man*, Vol.30, No.139, 1939.

Coggin Brown, J.C., "Note on Cinerary urns found in the Mundai country" in *Journal of Bihar and Orissa Research Society*, I, 1915.

Coghlam, H.H., *Notes on Prehistoric and Early Iron in the Old world*, Oxford, 1956.

Coon, C.S., *The Origin of Races*, New York, 1962.

Cunningham, A., *Ancient Geography of India*, Calcutta, 1924.

Cunningham, A., etc. *Comprehensive History of India*, Vol.II., Ed. Nilakanta Sastri.

Dani, A.H., *Prehistory and Protohistory of Eastern India*, Calcutta, 1960.

Das, B.M., A note on the races of Assam. In *Kamarupa*, B.M. Das (Ed.), Gauhati, 1967.

Deo, S.B., *Mahurjhari Excavation 1970-72*, 1973.

Dey, A.K., *Geology of India*, National Book Trust, India, New Delhi.

Dikshit, M.G., *Tripuri*, 1952.

Dikshit, M.G., *Some Beads from Kondapur*, Hyderabad Archaeological Series No.18, 1952.

Fingdon-F. Ward, *Plant Hunter in Manipur*, 1958.

F.A. Gait., *A History of Assam*, Revised edition 1963.

Garini, G.E.R., *Researches into Ptolemy's Geography*, 1968.

Ghosh, A.(Ed.), *Dictionary of Indian Archaeology.*

Ghosh, A.K., Prehistoric studies in Eastern India, *Science and Culture*, No.27, 1961.

Govt. of Manipur 1983. *A Report of the State Archaeology Department, Manipur:* Govt of Manipur.

Gopal, Lallanji, Antiquity of Iron in India, *Uttar Bharati,* Vol. IX, No.3.

Gunindro, P., *Epigraphic Records of Manipur,* Imphal, 1886

Hamilton, F.B., East India Gazetteer, 1915.

Hannay, S.F., Journey from the Capital of Ava to the Amber Mines of the Hulong Valley, vide 'Hill Tracts between Assam and Burma, 1873 and 1978'.

Hutton, J.H., Pre-history of Assam, *Man in India,* VIII(4) 1928:

Indian Archaeology 1978-79-A Review.

Indian Archaeology 1968-69-A Review.

Indian Archaelogy 1961-62-A Review

Indian Archaelogy 1965-66-A Review.

India, *A Regional Geography,* Ed. R.L.Singh, Varanasi, 1971.

Johnstone, J., *My experiences in Manipur and the Naga Hills,* London, 1896.

Jugeshwar Singh, L., Bhugol Ahanba, Impal, 1938; R.P. Singh, *Geography of Manipur,* N.B.T. Delhi,; M.A. Ansari, *Some Aspects of Geography of Manipur*

Kabui, G., *History of Manipur,* Vol.1, 1991. W.Yumjo Singh, *Report on Archaeological Studies in Manipur,* Imphal, 1935.

Kern, H., *Introduction to Brihatsamhita*

Kosambi, D.D., Culture and Civilization of Ancient India in Historical Outline, Delhi, 1970.

Kosambi, D.D., "The beginning of the Iron Age in India". *Journal of the Economic and Social History of the Orient,* Vol.VI, Pt.III (Leidon, 1963).

Krishnan, M.S., *Geology of India and Burma,* Madras, 1960.

Lahiri, A.N., 'A comparative account of noteworthy features of the Hindu coins of North Eastern India,' *Coinage and Economy of North Eastern States of India* (NSI, Varanasi).

Law, B.C., *Historical Geography of Ancient India,* Paris, 1954.

Martin, M., *Eastern India,* III, London, 1838.

Majumdar, R.C., Ancient Indian Colonies in the Far East, Vol. I, *Champa,* 1922.

Majumdar, R.C., *Age of Imperial Unity,* Vol.II.

Majumdar, R.C., *Expansion of Aryan Culture in East India,* Alombapur Memorial Lecture, Imphal, 1966.

Majumdar, R.C., *Ancient India as described by Classical Writers,* Calcutta, 1968.

Majumdar, R.C., *Hindu colonies in Far East.*

Mc Cosh, 'On the various lines of overland communications between India and China', P.R.G.S.

Mc Cuttoch, "Account of the Valley of Manipur. Selection from the records of the Government of India Foreign Department, No.XXIII, 1953.

Mc Crindle, *Ancient India as described by Ptolemy,* Calcutta, 1927.

Michell, *North-East Frontier of India.*

Montgomery, Martin, *The History, Antiquities, Topography and Statistics of Eastern India,* London, 1838.

Moti Chandra, *Arthasastra Trade and Trade Routes.* Book II, Chap XI in Ancient India, p.21.

Pargiter, F.E., Ancient countries in Eastern India, J.A.S.B., 1897

Patel, A.J., Pottery technique through the Ages, *Folklore,* Vol.IV., Nos.6-7, 1963.

Pemberton, R.B., *Report on the Eastern Frontier of British India,* 1835.

Phayrey, A.R., *History of Burma,* 1884

Proceedings of the Seminar on the Sources of History of Manipur and adjoining areas, Department of History, Manipur University, 1985.

Ramachandran, K.S., *A Bibliography of Indian Megaliths,* 1971.

Repson, E.J., *Cambridge History of India,* I, Delhi, 1955.

Risley, H.H., *The People of India,* Calcutta, 1915.

Roy, J., *A History of Manipur,* Calcutta, 1958

Sachau, E.C., *Alberuni's India,*- Vol.I

Sankalia, H.D., Spouted vessels from Navadatoli and Eran, *Antiquity,* Vol. XXIX, No.114, 1955.

Sankalia, H.D., and Deo, S.B., *Report on the Excavation at Nasik and Jorwe,* 1950-51, Poona, 1955.

Sankalia, H.D., and others *The Excavations at Maheshwar and Navadatoli,* 1952-53 Poona, Baroda, 1958.

Sankalia, H.D., etc. *From History of Prehistory at Nevasa,* Pune, 1960

Sarkar, S.S., *The Aboriginal races of India,* Calcutta, 1954.

Sarkar, D.C., *Studies in the Geography of Ancient and Medieval India,* Delhi, 1960.

Schoff, *Periplus of the Erythrean Sea.*

Sem, G., Mahabharata Asvamedha Parva; Goswami, H.C.: *Descriptive Catalogue of Assamese Manuscripts,* University of Calcutta, 1930, pp.99-100.

Shamasastry, R., *Arthasashtra,* Book II, Chap XI,1929.

Sharma, A.K., Sekta - The turning Point in *India Magazine,* New Delhi, March 1992.

Sharma, A.K & S.B. Ota, Excavation at Sekta (Manipur) 1991, in *Himalay-past and presednt,* Vol.II, 1991-92, (eds) M.P.Joshi, etc.

Sharma, A.K., 'Excavations at Ladyura' in *Puratattava* No.21, New Delhi, 1991

Sharma, A.K., *Emergence of Early culture in North-East India,* New Delhi, 1993

Sharma, A.K., Prehistoric Explorations in Sikkim in *Puratattava,* No.10, New Delhi, 1981.

Sharma, B.N., Unpublished Bronzes from Eastern India in The National Museum, New Delhi, *East and West,* Rome.

Sharma, B.K., Megalithic burials, Lohardanga, Dist. Ranchi, in *Indian Archaeology 1963-64 - A Review.*

Sharma, N.C., *Darrangraj Vamsavali,* Calcutta, 1973,

Sharma, T.C., 1986. Recent Archaeological discoveries in North-East India - Prehistoric period. Paper presented in South Asian Archaeological Congress held at New Delhi.

Sharma, T.C., *Pre-historic Archaeology of Assam - A study of Neolithic Cultures* Ph.D, Thesis, London University 1966 (Unpub)

Pre-historic Archaeology in North-Eastt India-A Review of Progress in *Eastern Himalayas* (ed Sharma and Majumdar), pp.102-35, New Delhi. 1980.

Singh, Ch. Manihar, The Meitei : Origin and Affinity, Journal of Manipur University, 1984.

Singh, L.I., *Introduction to Manipur,* Imphal, 1958

Singh, N. Khelchandra, *Ariba Manipurgi Sahitya Itihas,* 1969.

Singh, O., 1971. Purvanchal. *In India: A Regional Geography,* R.L. Singh (Ed.), Varanasi: National Geographical Society of India, pp 93-513.

Singh, O., Ibochuba, (Ed.). Bulletin of Mathura Museum, 1982.

Singh, O.K., Archaeological Researches in Manipur. In *Eastern Himalayas* (Ed.) T.C. Sharma and D.N. Majumdar, Cosmo Publications, Delhi. 1980.

Singh, O.K., Iconographs in Manipur. In *Scriptures of Manipur,* Mutua Museum Bull., No. 2. 1982.

Singh, O.K., 1983. Archaeology in Manipur -- Napachik; A stone Age site in the Manipur valley, Manipur, Govt. of Manipur.

Singh, O.K. & Sharma, T.C., Discovery of Stone Age Relics from Manipur *Jr. Assam* Sc. Sec. XII 36-48. 1969.

Singh, O.K., The Antiquities of Manipur, *Bull, Manipur State Museum* No.I, 1972: 1-10 Imphal. 1972.

A Report of the State Archaeology Deptt., Govt. of Manipur Imphal. 1983.

Singh., O.K., (1985) A Live Megalithic Culture in Manipur. In *Recent Advances in Indo-Pacific Prehistory,* (Ed) V.N. Misra and P. Bellwood, Oxford and IBH Publishing Co.

Singh, O.K., (1986) *Prehistoric Archaeology of Nongpok Keithelmanbi.* Amusana Institute of Antiquarian Studies, Manipur, Imphal.

Singh, O.K., and T.C. Sharma., On the Discovery of Stone Age Relics from Manipur, *Jr. Assam Science Society,* Vol.XII. 1969.

Singh, O.K., *Archaeology of Manipur,* Manipur: Govt of Manipur. 1988.

Singh, O.I., (Ed) *Coins of Manipur,* Muthua Museum Bull., No.1. 1980.

Singh, P.G., *Epigraphical Records of Manipur*

Singh, Jain Prakash, Sen Gupta & Gautam (Ed) *Archaeology of North-Eastern India,* New Delhi, 1991

Singh, Jhalajit, R.K., *A Short History of Manipur,* 1964

Singh, W. Yumjao., *Report on the Archaeological Studies in Manipur,* Bull. No.I, 1935, Imphal.

Sivaramamurti, C., *Early History of India,* Oxford, 1924.

S.K. Chatterjee, Kirata Jana Kriti, Contribution of Indo-Mongoloid people, Calcutta, 1950, 2nd Edition, 1974

Srivastava, B., *Trade and Commerce in Ancient India* (from earliest times to circa A.D. 300), Varanasi, 1906.

Srivastava, B.R., *Ancient Indian Trade and Trading Routes,* National Book Trust, India, New Delhi.

Stell, E.H., Celts found among the Namsang Nagas, *Proc. Asiatic Sec. Beng,* 1870, PP.267-68.

Subbarao, B., "*The Personality of India*", 1958.

Taylor, J., Journal of Asiatic Society of Bengal, 1, 1847.

Verrier Elwin, *India's North-East Frontier in the 19th Century*, 1954.

Wadia, D.N., *Geology of India,* 1939.

Warmington, E.H., *Commerce between Roman Empire and India,* Cambridge, 1928.

Watters, T., *On Yuan Chwang's Travels in India*, Delhi 1961, II.

Wheeler, Mortimer, *Early India and Pakistan.*

W. Robinson, *Descriptive Account of Assam,* Revised edition, 1963.

W. Yunja Singh, *Report on the Archaeological Studies of Manipur,* Manipur State Museum Bulletin, No.1, 1935.

INDEX